SUCCESS BEYOND
SPORT

How to Retire from Sport
& Keep Winning

Dear Laura,
Dare to dream
& Be Inspirational
Happy Birthday
Annette Huygens
2006

ANNETTE HUYGENS-THOLEN

Success Beyond Sport is a must-read for any successful athlete who has put blood, sweat and tears into his or her sport in order to be the very best but must, at some point, retire and become a "normal person". Acknowledging, understanding and taking action on this important transition starts well before retirement from sport and is vital to a happy and successful life where the lessons learned from World class competition can be effectively leveraged in a professional career.

• **SIMON ARKELL**
Two-time Olympian (Australia - Pole Vault)
Commonwealth Champion and record holder
Corporate CEO and Olympian Advisor, Five Ring Insight

Annette has tackled the fear, uncertainty and overwhelming responsibility that an athlete faces at the end of their sporting career, head on. Her 8 Winning Points and Success Training Exercises will guide you along your new journey as you begin to experience success off the sporting field. She will show you that when you retire from competition, you never have to retire from winning. This book will allow you to embrace your life beyond sport in a seamless and rewarding way.

• **NATALIE COOK**
4 time Olympian, 2000 Olympic Gold medallist

Annette hits some very key points that every athlete can relate to. Success beyond Sport gives very clear cut examples and strategies on how an athlete can transition from sport to the real world.

• **JOHN BRONSON**
Former tight-end for NFL Arizona Cardinals

Success beyond Sport has been extremely helpful in providing momentum and direction in the career search process that I am going through as a 42 year old. I have worked and trained most of my entire life, but I am at a very different stage in my life and your book has helped tremendously in providing the specific tools and encouragement to identify my goals, my skills, my passions, and ultimately my next career move. Thank you for taking the time to put this comprehensive and helpful book together to help all of the other athletes out there that are going through this difficult life-change in finding their way in life after sport and reminding these athletes of all of their transferrable skills that made them successful athletes in the their sport careers.

• ERICA WHEELER
1996 Olympian, Javelin

This is a subject that needs addressing! The interactive techniques Annette so clearly describes in this book apply to both the amateur and professional athlete and will help people carry over their peak performance skills and confidence from their athletic career to their professional career.

Annette is the perfect person to give the advice. Her vast experience as an Olympic athlete and many setbacks leading up to that point in her life give her the credibility needed to deliver such an insightful and worthwhile amount of coaching in this book.

• LISA GARR
Host, The Aware Show
Media Personality
Los Angles, California

Annette, thank you so much for writing such an awesome book. Now that I'm retired and I'm coaching other athletes in beach volleyball I can use this book as a very REAL reference on how to approach their journey in sport and beyond. A successful mind set is so crucial in life, not just in sport.

Anyone reading this will not only learn how to maximize their potential on the court while they are still playing, they will also have some fantastic tools to use upon retiring from sport and beginning a new career.

You have certainly captured the absolute essence of "winning" in a way that doesn't necessarily mean Gold. You've explained how people can win in life and win within themselves. Because, at the end of the day, it's all about being the best YOU can be.

You have written it with such honesty and directness that any retired athlete can identify with. I have had moments exactly like you've explained and would have loved to have read your book back then!

The lessons you've provided are spot on, however no one will ever really learn from any of them unless they decide to take ACTION right now.

Massive action equals massive results. Go for Gold.....

• KERRI POTTHARST
2000 Olympic Gold Medallist, 1996 Olympic Bronze Medallist
3 time Olympian

To the athletes who inspire so many with their dedication and commitment to excellence in sport.

Success Beyond Sport: How to Retire from Sport and Keep Winning
by Annette Huygens-Tholen

Love Your Life

Love Your Life Publishing, Inc
7127 Mexico Road Suite 121
St. Peters, Missouri USA 63376
800-930-3713

www.LoveYourLifePublishing,com

Cover and internal design: Sarah Barrie www.Cyanotype.ca

Printed in the United States of America and Australia.

ISBN: 978-1-934509-29-6
Library of Congress Control Number: 2009943107

•• TABLE OF CONTENTS ••

FOREWORD

• • BY CHRIS HOWARD • •

Christopher Howard Training has been researching and teaching the success strategies of the world's greatest minds for over a decade, and I've always said, "If I can do it, you can do it." So it truly heartens me to see Annette, a graduate of our training programs, take that message to heart. I've seen Annette grow from a student in my class to assisting at our major events and now teaching programs for Christopher Howard Training. I value the reputation of my companies, and I wouldn't put someone on my platform that didn't have the potential to be better than me.

As an Olympian, Annette has always demonstrated a commitment to do whatever it takes to succeed, and I know that she invested a lot in her own education, including joining our Billionaire Adventure Club. Unafraid to step up, it is this commitment that makes Annette such an inspirational role model for other former athletes. I have seen her transform from this person identifying herself with being a sportsperson to a gutsy, determined business woman, networking with some of the world's top business people.

The methods and program discussed in this book are the same principles we have used to help hundreds and thousands of individuals create the wealth and lifestyle they desire. Whether you are currently still competing in sport, planning to retire, or your sporting days are behind you, this book will show you how you can keep playing like a winner in everything that you do. Annette has added her own unique voice and experiences to impress upon you these valuable lessons that can in turn transform your life.

Our ability to create our own reality and therefore our results is a powerful tool that I have studied since my childhood. I know that by working with your goals, your beliefs, and your values, you will change. This book combines it all effectively to provide you with a self-help guide. Read about the winning points and do the exercises so that you too can move beyond the attachment to being a sportsperson. You are so much more than that.

You know, I love my sport – I can't live without my Brazilian Jiu-jitsu, and it's something I do almost daily, even when I'm on tour. But that is only something I *do*, and it's not who I *am*. When you read the section on *Identity,* you will also build a greater sense of who you are, and then there will be no stopping what you are capable of.

The mission of Christopher Howard Training is to empower individuals to live a deeply rich and fulfilling life, and I realized a long time ago that I couldn't do that on my own. I am so proud that Annette is getting this message out to you, and my hope is that you in turn will pass it forward so that all athletes can enjoy a successful and wealthy life beyond sport.

• Chris Howard
Lifestyle and Wealth Strategist,
Bestselling author: *Instant Wealth-Wake up Rich,*
and *Turning Passions into Profits.*

PREFACE

It is August 19, 2000 in Sydney, Australia, and the members of the Australian Olympic team are gathering in their area of the Olympic village. We are meeting there covered up with white raincoats so that any helicopters overhead won't be able to view us in our uniforms yet. They are to be a surprise when we finally enter the Olympic Stadium later that evening. The anticipation is high.

All of the Olympic teams make their way to the gymnastics stadium where we will wait and bide our time until our team is called upon. A small TV shows the telecast of the pomp and ceremony while we pass the hours meeting and greeting all the other athletes from a multitude of countries. What a beautiful sea of colors there is in the stadium with each country grouped together.

Then they start announcing country by country in alphabetical order to line up and start the procession towards the Olympic Stadium. As host country, Australia is last, so we watch the gymnastics stadium gradually empty, country by country, color by color, until it is our turn. We are one of the biggest contingencies, and as we line up Andrew Gaze, our country's team captain and flag bearer, is running up and down along the ranks with the Australian flag. He is so excited that it's contagious, lighting us all up with excitement and anticipation.

It is a long procession towards the Olympic Stadium, and we make our way like a snake towards the tunnel, still another 20-30 minutes away. As we wind our way towards the cauldron, all the athletes are hustling for the best position. We want to be near the outside so that the camera can see us. My dad, my sister, my niece, and my dad's partner aren't able to be at the ceremony, but I know they will be watching on TV. We move to be in a good spot so our families can see us.

We are on the outside as we stand in the tunnel waiting to march in, listening to hear our country being called. The excitement and anticipation builds within us, until finally they call "Australia!" My beach volleyball partner, Sarah Straton, and I grab each other's hands, celebrating this moment...we have done it, we are here!

It was one of the proudest moments in my life. My childhood dream was to go the Olympics. From the age of nine, I devoted my life to sport, first as a gymnast and then as a volleyball player. With persistence and determination, I made it. There I was living my dream. I still get goose bumps as I think of walking through that tunnel and emerging to be in front of 100,000 people cheering us on. As we walked around, we threw out little rubber kangaroos and waved vigorously to everyone in the crowd. The energy of so many people swept us around the Olympic Stadium rejoicing in what we had done.

Then it was all over.

After September 2000, after the street parades and all the fanfare had subsided, my life completely changed. I was retired.

I thought I was ready for the transition because I had some vague ideas and desire to pursue sports marketing or media, but my biggest post-Olympic goal was just to be "normal," which meant to me, settle down, have a home, stay in one place and BE HAPPY. Have you heard that one before? "I just want to be happy!"

Well, it took me six long years and three attempts to retire from sport! It was a very confusing and disheartening period of transition. The first time I retired was because I had reached my goal of playing in the Olympics and thought there was nothing left to do in the sport. I was trying to move forward but had nothing compelling enough to strive for so I kept going back to playing volleyball because it was what I loved and thought it was the only thing I was good at. The second time I retired was because I thought I was getting old at age 37 and should take care of my back. Screws had held my back together since '92, and I was keen to maintain myself in good condition until my old age.

When I retired for the third time in early 2007 at age 41, it was finally for the right reasons—I had new goals that filled me with greater passion. Having a positive direction to move toward inevitably provides the type of empowering motivation that produces results.

After six years of aimlessness, I once again had clear direction and inspiration. I became, once again, a goal-seeking missile. I was not only setting personal and professional goals for myself, I was achieving them quicker and faster than ever before. My life was back on track, my new sense of purpose stronger than ever before. I now realized that there was so much more for me to accomplish and create in life than just making it to the Olympics. This is what finally convinced me to put away the competition swimsuit for good.

A whole new future was opening up for me. All that I studied and learned during that time of transition got me playing a much bigger game. When I suddenly retired from international competition with no clear idea of what I wanted to do next, I struggled. It doesn't have to be that way for you! I am going to teach you in this book all the winning techniques that completely changed my life.

INTRODUCTION

I spent the majority of my life focused on one dream—the dream of going to the Olympics. Yes, I made it. That tiny seed of an idea... that someday I would participate in that spectacular, international arena was planted in my mind when I was ten years old as I watched the opening ceremonies on TV. That vision for my future took root and finally came to fruition when I represented Australia in beach volleyball at the Sydney Olympics in 2000. But I also experienced post-Olympic blues, a period of years after I stopped playing professionally and before I had any new compelling goals. It was a tough time. I felt lonely, isolated, and lacking direction.

I am now an International Speaker and Master Results Coach, using the methodology of Neuro-linguistic programming and other techniques to transform people's behaviors and results. Realising that other athletes may experience the same struggle as I did, I devised an 8-step program called *Success beyond Sport* to teach the important keys that enabled me to transform my life and to help others transition successfully to new and fulfilling careers.

The Problem

Career athletes can hit a wall when their time on the field or in the limelight is over. Whether, their time is cut short by an injury or age, there is always a time when athletes must transition from one type of sporting field to the playing field of life and a career beyond sport.

Since the basis of their identity is wrapped up with being an athlete, it can create confusion, a lack of direction, and a lack of purpose in their minds. This mindset can cause retired athletes to feel down and anxious. Some even suffer depression. After having a career that brought so much reward, they now feel unfulfilled— emotionally and perhaps financially.

These negative feelings can cause athletes to get stuck. They become helpless and unmotivated to find a new way to fulfill their needs and desires to excel and succeed. Others find a job to fill their time and pay their bills, but the work may not be fulfilling to them. All of this challenges the retired athlete's self-esteem and even the meaning of life.

I have identified, through my own experience and research, several factors that contribute to an athlete's fall from the highs and glory of their sporting career into his or her so called after-life. For any individual it could be one or two of these factors or all of them contributing to the difficulties in transitioning to a new career. These factors include, but are not limited to,

1. **A loss of significance.** Significance is recognized as a human need and can be lost when athletes finish playing sport. People will actively seek to fulfill their needs, either consciously or unconsciously, and the significance can be relative to one (e.g. being significant in a relationship) or relative to many, (e.g. media attention). Significance can be attained positively or negatively.

2. **A lack of new inspiring goals.** Athletes are commonly renowned for goal seeking and goal achievement. Goals are key to providing motivation and direction. It is not uncommon for ath-

letes to forget to set new goals with the same dedication and commitment on retirement from sport. For some, retiring from sport is about 'not playing sport' rather than looking forward and toward what is next.

3. A loss of self-belief. Successful athletes have a committed and persistent attitude to their goals because of a belief that they can do it. Sometimes, this self-belief does not translate easily to skills outside of sport. Athletes might believe that their talents and abilities are limited to the sports arena. Until they apply the same commitment and persistence to everything they desire to do, they will struggle to achieve the same level of success.

4. Loss of support. Athletes lose more than the activity of sport when they retire. They also lose team-mates, coaches, and all those involved in helping the athlete to succeed. Who is there to support them now in a new career environment?

5. Lack of new skills. Athletes train almost daily on perfecting the skills and techniques required for their particular sport. Some skills, such as team-work and time-management, are transferrable to new areas, and there are likely to be new resources and skills required for their new career. It may take time, study, investment to develop these, but it is necessary not only to achieve new success but to feel fulfilled in the new career. It is said that if you are not learning, then you are dying.

6. Lack of a game plan. Action needs to be taken for goals to be achieved and ideally a plan will determine what actions need to be taken and when. Many people do not plan and then wonder why they are not getting anywhere. Athletes are used to having a schedule to fit in all their training commitments as well as other aspects of their life.

7. Strong identity with sport and the past. A life committed to sport can result in a strong identification as an athlete or sportsperson. Rather than looking forward towards a new career, retired athletes might find themselves looking to the past at how they were, and what they did achieve. Identity determines the behavior of an individual and therefore their results.

Many of the difficulties of transition relate to the mindset of the individual and how prepared they were for life after sport. In my experience, it doesn't matter how prepared one is, the reality is still a shock. Going from being a winner in the sports arena to a rookie in the business world, often starting from scratch, is challenging to one's self-esteem.

I know how tough it can be to face life after sport. Looking back at those transitional years, I reflect that I was floating at sea on a course to nowhere. Prior to 2000, the only dream I had ever really had was to compete at the Olympic Games, and that one goal had spurred me on through all the highs and lows. Unfortunately, after the Games, I did what many athletes do upon reaching their dreams...I didn't set new ones. I didn't reset my path. I didn't know what to do next, so I sort of just muddled along, wandering wherever the path took me. I kept going back to my past. I went back to using my physiotherapy degree, which didn't excite me and wasn't fulfilling. Instead, I just kept going back to beach volleyball because that's what I knew and loved.

It wasn't just the change of lifestyle. It was that I stopped doing the things that had enabled me to create my success in the first place. I had the ability to achieve whatever I set my mind to, yet, I didn't know exactly how I had done it, and even if I did know, I would have been clueless as to how to apply them in "the real world." I had more skills than I was aware of at the time, and I had no idea how to transfer my success to business or apply my training to a new career. What I didn't realize then—and you have the opportunity to learn now—is that the same winning principles I used for decades on the volleyball court, also apply to the game of life!

The Solution

Consider this book your training manual of the mind for you to succeed in any field. Whether you play football, badminton, cricket, or soccer or swim, run, or wrestle, there is a certain psychological preparation needed before getting out on that field to win. It most often includes training so consistently that you feel confident, that you've built the necessary skills and developed the footwork so you're on top of your game, and there's nothing more to do but get out there and play. You do your best. The results you get—how you score, how you personally perform, how the team works together, your mental and emotional mindset going in—all depend on a set of variables. It's that success mindset, the mental resourcefulness that this book develops through its focused **Success Training Exercises.**

As athletes, we have first-hand experience of how much our mindset can affect our game. Still, most of our athletic training is just physical. Through repetitive exercises and hours, weeks, years upon years of practices, we hone our bodies' skills. This book and my program works in much the same way—you practice the *8 Winning Points* to prepare yourself and your mind to achieve the same level or better success in life as you enjoyed in sport.

I've found in my career as an Olympic volleyball player that too many of us let our emotions and our thoughts get the better of us out there on the field. That's where the real game happens—within the mind! This inner game determines whether we're "on" or whether we're "off" our game.

The sad part is that very few athletes feel they have a good handle on how to manage their inner performance. They are at the mercy of where their emotions take them, too often to their detriment. Emotions and thoughts also affect results in business, relationships and all areas of life. Managing the mind and emotional states plays a huge part in winning. Consistent scorers tend to keep their internal states in check.

This 8 Point program for achieving anything you desire is a unique approach to career training. You can use this system to alter and develop every component of your thinking, including decisions, beliefs, values, attitudes, and emotional states. These are the components of the mind that ultimately determine your outcomes. You will be able to train yourself to act and react in a way that can consistently get you what you want. Whether you are still playing or already retired and transitioning into life after sport, you will find in these chapters the information you need to upgrade your skills, knowledge, and life purpose. This set of tools and practices can be used to succeed in the field of business, finance, relationships, effective communication, leadership, and any other area where you want to improve your performance.

This isn't a book about mind control. It's about expanding the capacity of your inner resources so that you can utilize them when and where you need them. It is about knowing the psychology behind success so you catch yourself when you're going down a losing road, and know exactly how to turn any moment around to your advantage. I present 8 separate principles that are all interconnected in the same way that you might go through the separate phases of sport training or competition to build your strength, your fitness and your flexibility. This program progressively prepares you to go out there and rock the house, no matter where you find yourself in life at any given moment.

You Can Change!

How often have you heard, or even used, the excuse, "That's just how I am!" Well, no more! You don't have to resign yourself to being the way you currently are. If the way you are is not serving you, then you can take steps to make changes, even create a new you. Our mind is a wondrous and flexible thing, and once we become aware of thoughts, behaviors and even values that are limiting us, we can go about changing them. You can set your own targets, design your own end game, write your own set of rules, even create a new identity more suited to who you want to be and what results you want to achieve.

Athletes have so many skills and so much passion to succeed in anything they set their minds to, but they have to know what they want and how to use their abilities to get there. I see my job is to wake them up to that. My dream now is to help others, people just like you, who perhaps do not yet realize how great they can be.

I've lived through it and realize that it's not easy changing careers. It's a challenge going from doing something that you love and are good at, to finding something new. It's not easy going from being a star (at any level) to a life of mediocrity, so don't do it. Why aim for mediocrity when you can aim to be the best in something new?

How to Use This Book

I am a student, teacher, and coach of the mindset of success and how the unconscious mind affects results. There is so much to learn from the habits of the past. I found that some of my habits served me, and some didn't. By exploring these, it has enabled me to utilize my strengths and work on new ones in order to move forward. I begin each chapter with a personal story from my own sporting career journey, how I fulfilled my dream of playing in the Olympic Games, and more importantly, how I transformed my own thinking and approach to life to enjoy a new fulfilling career as a Coach, Speaker, and Entrepreneur, using these same 8 key steps. Use the Success Training Exercises in this book to transform you from a champion in sport to a champion in life.

The stories don't always follow a chronological timeline but are used to emphasize one of the progressive lessons. The Winning Points and Success Training Exercises are arranged progressively to strengthen and empower your mindset much like an athlete goes from pre-season training, through the regular season to build towards a Podium Finish in life. So if the program looks familiar, it's because the steps, the philosophy, and the process you followed during your sporting career are similar—you will be able to put this system into practice in any new environment.

My intent is that, by sharing these keys, you will never have to struggle in your transition into life beyond sport. Whether you chose to retire or the decision was forced upon you, these steps will help you focus forward and make your success easier to accomplish. You can continue to progress in your career quickly and efficiently, or you can keep doing what you're doing, it's up to you. Live your dream, or keep turning the wheel. It's time to let go of your past and open your mind to something new, so you can learn how to reach higher goals and fulfill the bigger dream. Are you ready?

THE OLYMPIAN ARCHETYPE

The Olympian is a stunning archetype with roots in the realm of the gods. Mythically, the Olympians are a group of 12 immortals who live in a palace on Mount Olympus, from which they took their name. What is it about the Olympian that sets them apart from others? What is the difference between the Olympian and the Athlete? These archetypes are not confined to sport, but rather are patterns of power that are lived in every aspect of life.

When someone describes the consistent prowess of an athlete, the images that come to mind are of a healthy body achieved through stamina, endurance, dedication. The Athlete embodies elements of power and vitality. A person can approach life with athletic vigor and never take to a sporting field or event. The qualities required to succeed in life, wherever applied, may well have athletic proportions. Some who read this may recognize the effort it has taken them to have a successful business, career, relationship, or even health. The ability to overcome physical limitations and endure, where others may have given up long before, speaks clearly of the athlete.

Then add the dimension of the Olympian. It is not to say that the Athlete does not have spirit; the Olympian, however, has it in spades. Olympians know and embody the stamina of the athlete; it is not without effort that they excel, but it is the talent that when you see it on full display is somehow not of this earth. The Olympian somehow embodies that something mythical that oozes from the mountain top, and it is no coincidence that this is also the origin of ethics, from the Greek word *Ethos*. As a context, in the realm of sporting prowess, it is the Olympians who are held to the highest standards; the consequences of dishonoring the code of ethics of the Olympic Flag are unforgiving. The standards held are reflected in the consequences when an Olympian falls from grace.

So what of these champions once they leave their chosen arena? What happens following unearthly accomplishments? In speaking with Olympians (be they of the sporting variety or the bastions of business) since turning my attention wholeheartedly to the study of archetypes and their patterns of power in our lives, one quandary is consistently true—what to do when you come crashing back down to earth?

When the reality of the peak of Olympic fitness is past, and the lofty heights of success are behind you. Where to next? This can be a journey that is both heartbreaking and exhilarating, but it is in the spirit of the Olympian that you'll understand the path that may have once looked so literal is now symbolic and pervasive. The altitude at which Olympians live their lives in every moment speaks of choices and actions that shape and reshape their lives constantly. A friend of mine wrote, "The Olympian ultimately shows us 'the power of unity over the divisiveness of competition.'"

The Olympian shows us what is humanly possible when
you work with the Gods.

• Written by Bronwyn Boyle
Archetypal Consultant
www.bronwynboyle.com

CHAPTER ONE

PRE-SEASON TRAINING

"We are made wise not by the recollection of our past, but by the responsibility for our future."

• George Bernard Shaw

It All Started With A Dream

I've loved sport ever since I can remember. From a very early age, something within me burned to be active, to strive, to achieve. At primary school, I always looked forward to the athletic season. I clearly recall my very first school's sports day—it was not an illustrious start to my career. At five or six years of age, I got confused about which group I was meant to be with to march to the school oval and found myself marching straight off in the wrong direction with the group that was not participating in the races! I was so disappointed to miss out on the opportunity to run and compete that day.

I did learn from my mistake though. The next year, I made absolutely sure I would race. As it turned out, I was actually pretty fast, though not the fastest. Throughout my years of primary school I was a constant second to another girl in my age group.

When I was seven, I also dreamed of being a ballet star. My grandmother, Oma, had come to live with us from The Netherlands when I was three years old, and my sister and I would always check to see what Oma was watching on television at night in case it was better than what Mum and Dad were watching. We could always count on Oma watching some variety show, and I enjoyed watching the ballet with her. So my parents allowed me to take ballet and tap classes.

I loved it, but one day my teacher suggested that I might be better suited to gymnastics. I'm so glad she did! I was a little too athletic for ballet. Tumbling and walking along the balance beam suited me so much better. That was the start of my dedicated sporting life. I looked forward to class every week and started to get focused on regularly practiced gymnastics routines. I was quickly rising through advanced levels, winning all of my earlier club level tests and excelling on the floors and beam...this was also when Nadia Comaneci wowed the world with her perfection during the 1976 Olympic Games in Montreal. I was ten.

Those were the first Olympic Games I took an interest in and really understood, particularly the gymnastics competition. I also recall being absolutely mesmerized by the opening and closing ceremonies. That was the moment my dream began...I would be a part of that opening ceremony and someday compete in the Olympics.

Nadia had been the first gymnast to ever be awarded a perfect score of ten in an Olympic gymnastics event. That fact struck me very deeply. A girl from Romania, with a name which meant "hope," had transformed my idea of what it meant to have a goal. She had begun her gymnastics career in kindergarten with a local team called "Flame." At the age of only six, she had been chosen to attend Bela Karolyi's experimental gymnastics school. She eventually became the youngest gymnast ever to win the Romanian Nationals. I was in awe of everything she had done. I remember hearing how the scoreboards at the Olympics hadn't even been equipped to display Nadia's scores of a perfect "10.0." Her marks were so high that they had to be reported as "1.00." My dream became to be like Nadia.

Over the course of the Olympics that year, Nadia Comaneci earned six additional perfect scores of ten and eventually captured three gold medals, one silver and one bronze. I was greatly inspired and motivated by this tremendous athletic achievement. As I progressed through the gymnastic levels, tests, and competitions, I regularly demonstrated to be one of the better gymnasts in Queensland for my level.

It did not always go my way, however. One of my more disappointing moments came when I was around eleven or twelve. Our coach had planned a tour to the USA to practice with the American gymnasts and coaches, visiting clubs in Reno, Nevada. As a member of the more elite squad in the club, I fully expected to be considered for the trip. It was a bitter setback when the team was announced, and I was the only one of our group to miss out! Two gymnasts younger than I with less experience received the nod ahead of me. It was a disappointing surprise, and I was highly jealous of my five friends who were given the opportunity. It was the first time I was challenged to deal with the sense of not being good enough in the eyes of a coach. Because of the situation, I decided at this point that life was not always fair. But I also discovered an inner fortitude within myself I didn't know I had. At such a young age, this first setback could have led to my giving up. It is interesting to look back and recognize that my response to the situation was a resourceful one—despite not being chosen for the team, I didn't assume I wasn't good enough. Instead, I dug my heels in to work even harder to prove myself. It became an opportunity to get better at my game.

Decisions Affect Results

Start to think about what decisions you have made in the past that have gotten you results you wanted, and others you did not want. What decisions you are making now about your future or your ability to achieve your set goals? They will determine what actions, or inactions, you make or don't make.

I will toss a lot of concepts at you right off the bat that may challenge your current way of thinking to stretch and strengthen your mind for great performance capacity in your life. That is the whole point. You are where you are right now because of the actions and decisions you've made up until now...if you want different results, or you want to get to where you want to go further and faster, you have to first become conscious of what type of thinking has gotten you here.

So I am introducing you to a whole system of interconnected concepts that will serve as your foundation to develop a winning mindset. Consider that I'm you're coach and this next set of principles and exercises is your pre-season prep. That entails training your mind to think in new ways. Stay open-minded and ready to think on your feet because this is not your average physical warm-up session. This program is designed to allow you to face any challenge with confidence, to overcome weaknesses that may have held you back before in your game, and, ultimately, allow you to rise to any occasion on any field or court—including the playing field of life—to be at your optimal performance at all times.

I went skiing one year up in the Andes Mountains. I had only a day, and I was determined to learn how to ski so I could enjoy a good long run on the beginner's mountain slope. I started with an hour's lesson, and pretty soon I was falling down quite regularly. It was part of the learning process. Luckily, the instructor had already shown me how to fall properly. Even though he was there to teach me how to stay on my feet, I learned quickly that it was okay to fall, and I would be safe.

As your coach, my intention is for you to know that, even in the face of failure, you will be safe as you move forward because you will have the inner strength and strategies to prevail and win. Making decisions is a basic foundational skill that will drive you forward and enable you to turn any seeming negative into a positive. The ability to respond from a position of power, knowing that you alone determine your own results, gives you an advantage whether you're launching a new career, or taking your professional game to the next level. This is because your decisions influence what actions you take, which determines the results you get:

As an example of how the decisions we make can affect our outcomes, let me share another story with you that occurred during my athletic career and how it affected my life. When I started out playing beach volleyball on the World Tour in 1994, the sport was relatively new internationally. Australia had one of the strongest competitions, after Brazil and the USA. My partner at that time, Kerri Pottharst, and I found quick success. By the end of 1994, we were ranked 8th in the world and gaining momentum.

Relationships play an important role in any sport but are especially intense and pivotal in beach volleyball where you are a two-person team. My volleyball partnership was increasingly strained at a time when Kerri and I were starting to assert ourselves as the number one team for Australia. While we were on track to qualify for the Atlanta Olympic Games—the first time Beach Volleyball would be an Olympic sport—Kerri opted to switch partners and play with Natalie Cook instead.

This was a serious setback for me with the 1994 Olympic Games right around the corner. Though initially disappointed, I knew I couldn't waste time blaming anyone for the situation in which I found myself. My goal was still within my view, if not within my reach. I just needed to come up with a new partner to continue on my quest for Olympic representation. I considered three choices, and without rushing into things, chose to move interstate from Perth (WA) to Sydney (NSW) to join up with another player. This was the first of several moves I would make over the next seven years in pursuit of a playing partner and my dream to compete at the Olympics.

During this same period of time before the Games when Kerri split with me, other teams were changing also. There was another high-ranked player who found herself in a similar situation—dumped! In her search for a teammate, we briefly talked of playing together; however, I decided the Sydney player was my better option. Despite her enormous talent, that player never did return to competitive beach volleyball after that. I believe it was her first-ever big setback and she didn't quite have the tools—the mental and emotional resources—to deal with it in a way that moved her forward in her career. I understand from others that she felt betrayed by the players, the coaches and the whole professional volleyball system, believing: "It wasn't fair!"

Now, I'm not saying her life is any better or worse for that decision. She just chose to go down a completely different from the path she initially chose, a very different from the path I took by taking responsibility for my own success and moving on to put together a great team.

Consider the following statements:

"I am <u>successful</u> because of the challenges in my life."

"I am <u>unsuccessful</u> because of the challenges in my life."

Two people can have the exact same challenge in their lives and have two vastly different thought processes about what the circumstance *means,* what they imagine it signifies to them personally. They can then make entirely different decisions about how to react to the situation, and therefore, get different outcomes. We've all heard uplifting stories of impoverished individuals growing up facing truly daunting challenges that would stop most people in their tracks, who go on to defy the odds and become very wealthy. We've also probably all listened to individuals who regale us with stories about how "hard" life is, how "broke" they are, and how "impossible" it is to get ahead. These are the ones who will likely never make anything more of their lives than what they believe because they've already decided it's useless, and therefore, don't bother to make the effort toward what they do want.

It is not the challenges that determine your results; it is what you do about those challenges.

Emotions Affect Decisions

Now let's back up a step and ask ourselves, "So, if the decisions we make determine our results, then what is it that determines our decisions?

Well, compare the decisions you make when you are feeling sad or upset to the decisions you make when you feel happy and optimistic.

For example, you're driving a car one day and end up sitting in peak-hour traffic. You're feeling great, so you decide to turn on the radio and nothing can change how you're feeling. You just listen to the music, and it doesn't matter about the peak-hour traffic. You arrive at work still in a good mood. The next day, you hit the same traffic, but this time you got up on the wrong side of the bed or you got news from the office that puts you in a lousy mood…suddenly you're going in and out of traffic, changing lanes, maybe driving more aggressively than is safe, and letting your bad mood negatively affect your interactions with colleagues when you finally get to work. Whether your behavior got you to your destination faster is questionable. What's unquestionable is that your emotions (how you feel) affected your reactions, which changed your outcome.

Start to become aware of how your emotions lead you to make decisions that may or may not be empowering or effective in getting you where you want to go. When I use the term "empowering," I mean consciously responding in a way that moves you toward what you want. How do you know if you're heading for success? Ask yourself:

- *Do I feel motivated by my choices?*
- *Do I feel that I determine my own actions?*
- *Or am I reacting to events around me, just hoping that I happen to get it right someday?*
- *What steps am I taking now to make sure that I am in an optimal state to get the most out of my day? My year? My life?*

A surprising number of people don't even realize they can choose their responses. It would seem emotions are just a natural response to the outside world over which we have little to no control. How can you influence your feelings or emotions to produce better actions and therefore results? Can we choose how we respond?

Yes, you can choose how to respond to any situation! I will discuss in a later chapter how you can take greater control of your emotional state. For the meantime, it is important to understand the effect that your emotional states have on your behaviors:

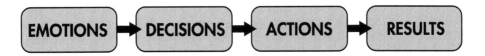

Competitive sport can be a rollercoaster of emotion if you let it —you're on the top of the world one day, sunk to the depths the next—and as we all know these ever-changing states can effect our performance, for better or for worse. The trick to getting off that rollercoaster to demonstrate more consistent results is taking charge of the *meanings* you initially create in your mind.

An emotion may seem to arise automatically. Actually, an emotional state comes from the thought process that preceded it. That doesn't mean you have to act on it. You just have to become conscious first of what those deeper thoughts are that are generating your reactions. Then, you can simply DECIDE to respond differently. You can actually alter the emotion by shifting the way you perceive the event that gave rise to the emotion.

Meaning Affects Emotions

Awareness is the necessary first step before any change can occur. By being aware of your emotional state, you can start to consider whether the emotion can serve a purpose or not. You can interrupt the habitual response and, instead, respond deliberately and consciously.

I will talk more about emotions later, but for now, when feeling negative, consider asking yourself:

- *Why am I feeling this way?*
- *What did (the incident or statement) mean to me in order for me to feel this way?*

Emotions serve as a guidance system to help us. It's a good idea to listen to them. If you are angry or sad, it guides you to consider that something about a situation does not sit well with you. For example, does the anger of being dropped from a team make you want to quit? Or does it spur you on? Does missing a shot make you more focused? Or do you tell yourself you're not good enough?

For example, if you choose to think it means "sports is unfair" then you're not going to want to continue in the field because it's not in line with who you are. If you choose to believe that a partner dropped you and that means, "Now I have the opportunity to find a better match for me," then you will be empowered to do just that. By being conscious of the meaning you apply to situations you can have more control over your emotional states and make better decisions.

I believe what we achieve in sport and in life is a reflection of how we conduct ourselves. Our performance usually suffers when we approach conditions reactively. The times that we sometimes slip and act as if we have no control over our emotions, our actions or our results, we relinquish responsibility and quickly find ourselves at a disadvantage. For example, the meaning you give to a particular challenge—"it's impossible" versus "it is possible"—will determine how you feel about that challenge—hopeless versus determined. This is the difference between disempowering and empowering decisions that determine your actions.

Always go for the empowering thought over the disempowering one.

Everyone has the ability to choose the meaning given to any particular situation. Sometimes you may feel like there is no choice, only because your choices have become habits, often ingrained from your early childhood years. Sometimes the choice seems so logical or obvious that you wouldn't consider that other options exist. Here is where many a disagreement or argument arises, because someone is unable to see that there can be different meanings attributed to the same situation. Most people are caught up in their own meaning, mistaking it for the truth.

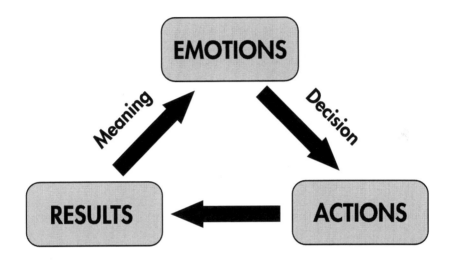

By accepting that your truth is not THE truth and considering alternative points of view, you can start to look at situations differently. Putting a positive "spin" on an event would lead to you feeling differently about the situation. You would then act differently, and therefore, produce different results.

When you're training for a competition and your coach has you focus on changing one small bad habit you've developed over the years… that one change can make the difference between winning and not winning. If you *only* applied this same focus to changing your mental habits - making more empowered meanings, it could alter your performance 100% at work, in relationships and in sport.

Taking it from the other direction, if you are not getting the results you want in life, start by changing the meaning you have given to that particular area of your life. For example, if you're not happy with missing out on getting a job, instead of thinking you're not good enough, start thinking about what you can do differently to secure the next job. Perhaps it *means* the job was not right for you and that there are better jobs suited to your qualifications. Notice how this change in perspective actually begins to transform the outcomes you get in this area.

Have you ever been in a game and an opponent gives you certain look that you cannot interpret and you assume it's negative? Or they are actually rude and it makes you think about past interactions that were unpleasant and you let it throw you off your entire game? Or maybe it made you play more aggressively and beat them? What if you then discovered that something distressful had happened to that other player the night before? Perhaps they had experienced a loss in the family or a relationship break-up. How would you feel about him/her then? Would you behave differently? This is another phenomenon that occurs in sports teams all the time—you can end up reacting to their reaction, which triggers emotional reactions in the rest of the team...all based on misinterpretations! So watch what you're saying to yourself in your own mind...it could cost you your next game, or your whole career.

Facing Down Failure

"I missed more than 9,000 shots in my career. I've lost over 300 games. I've failed over and over in my life. And that is also why I succeed."
                                        • Michael Jordan

"Failures" can define our futures...in whatever way we let them. Circumstances are just events devoid of meaning. We decide what meaning to give them, how we want to respond to them...and this in time can decide our destiny. To illustrate this point, I would like to continue my personal story where I left off...

I was in the middle of a run of successes at state-level gymnastics, rapidly moving up to level seven out of ten when a major perceived stumbling block interrupted my journey. Not only did I not finish high in the competition to get to next level, I did not even pass! I failed! I could barely come to grips with not being the best. It was extremely upsetting to watch all my friends go on ahead of me. I was not coping well with the greater levels of difficulty that were included in the higher-level compulsory routines.

Perhaps it was due to growth spurts, but it took me three attempts to pass level seven. I did persist though, and the extra work I put in made my body stronger. Soon enough, I found myself once again on the winner's podium.

In 1979 I made my first Queensland representative team in the under-14 division, and traveled to Perth with a team of six others, finishing with the second highest score for the team. Our top scorer, Kelly Wilson, finished fourth overall and would go on to represent Australia with distinction, including at the 1984 Olympic games.

I repeated the result the next year at junior level, narrowly missing selection in the Australian squad of fifteen. That same year, I competed in the Australian national level 9 competition, where I made apparatus finals in beam and floor. Unbeknownst to me at the time, that was to be my last year of full competition. In 1981, I started to be plagued by back problems that got progressively worse despite physiotherapy and rest.

My future in gymnastics came to a crashing halt at one state competition where I broke down after a bars routine. During my dismount I wrapped around the bars and the forced pressure was just too much for my already weakened spine. X-rays showed that I had in fact been born with congenital defects of the spine. Where five vertebrae of my lower spine should have been fused, one was not. The disc with it was inadequate to properly support my spine.

Adding to the problem was a diagnosed case of "spina bifida occulta." This is a mild form of spina bifida where the spine of one vertebrae is incomplete, not joining at the back. The spina bifida occulta was not a problem on its own, and many people have this condition without being aware. In more serious cases, this congenital defect leaves a serious hole exposing the spinal cord and rendering the newborn a paraplegic. My mother recalled that I had been born with a tiny "weeping hole" in my skin at the base of my spine, which had quickly healed. How fortunate I was to have ever even been able to perform gymnastics or any other sport! Unfortunately, these defects combined with the injury from gymnastics impaired my body's ability to heal.

Initially that was all the X-rays revealed, but in later years they picked up the stress fractures that I had sustained through the rigorous gymnastics training. With the gift of hindsight, I should never have been able to participate in gymnastics at such a competitive level. I am so grateful that I did though as I see the skills I learned, both mentally and physically, served as the foundation for my later success in professional volleyball.

When I was at a very young age, gymnastics honed my discipline to train and fuelled my ambition to succeed in competitive sport. I had succeeded through persistence and dedication. My initial reaction to having to quit gymnastics was devastation. It had been my life, and it was difficult to imagine life without it. My mind turned very quickly, though, to searching for what I could do next. I started asking myself, "If I can't do gymnastics, what other sport could I participate in? What sport would I excel in?...*How could I still go to the Olympics?*"

Turn Failure Into Feedback

Everybody has challenges in life. It is how you choose to deal with those challenges, that distinguishes who you become and what you can accomplish.

To illustrate further how the meaning you give to events determines the results you get in life, let's consider a situation athletes can relate to. When making quick decisions on the field or having to make big career decisions on an ongoing basis—an athlete may, on occasion, feel a sense of "missed opportunity." This can be a tough one psychologically. It can be difficult to deliberately *choose* your response when you may be overwhelmed in the moment, either by the disappointment of a missed goal or with a feeling that a winning game career opportunity so narrowly passed you by.

One may choose to see an opportunity passed up as a "failure." You can also switch mental gears to very quickly recognize the situations as feedback—by "feedback" I mean, information that you can learn from and use to move forward. Viewing it as a "failure" can easily turn one missed opportunity into a downward cycle of future missed opportunities.

To only see a "loss" as being a failure is to hit a wall. To see it as an opportunity for further gain is an open door to much bigger wins down the road!

Think of a circumstance that you believe was a negative turn of events and ask yourself:

- *What is it that I can do NOW so that I can turn a temporary setback into a success?*

Disempowering cycle

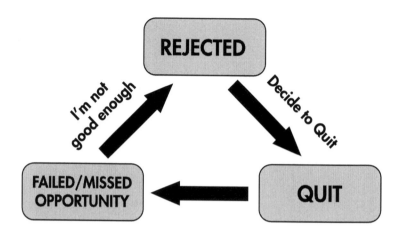

Empowering cycle

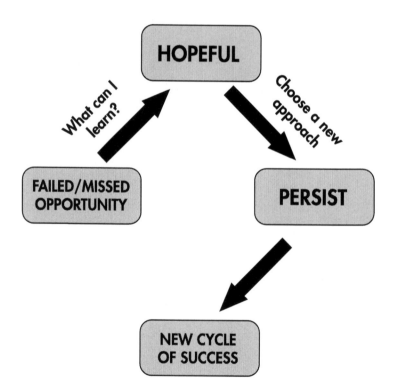

· ·

WINNING POINT #1:
Take Responsibility

"You must take personal responsibility. You cannot change the circumstances, the seasons, or the wind, but you can change yourself."

• Jim Rohn

Take Control of the Ball

To be "responsible" is to "be accountable for one's actions and decisions." But how can we be accountable if we are not even consciously aware of what decisions we are making at any given moment?

One of the first foundational skills to achieve success in any field is to be 100% accountable for your experience at all times. Accountability gives you your game advantage in every situation. When I was told I had three separate spinal problems, it didn't knock me off my game for very long. Instead of using that as a reason or excuse to quit, I chose not to interpret that to mean, "You'll never make it to the Olympics. You don't have what it takes." I instead asked myself, "Well then, what do I have to do so I *can* get to the Olympics?" I switched gears and started looking for other options that were open to me. I've heard it said, "When one door closes, another one opens."

Taking personal responsibility for the results you get is where all your power will come from in your career and in sport.

Events and other players will always come along to knock you off your footing. But a good coach doesn't allow you to come off a losing match and blame the other team for being better or having all the luck. In life, as in sport, a champion takes responsibility for everything. If you're pointing the finger at all the other players and circumstances you think are preventing you from reaching your goals, then you have let go of the ball. You cannot score unless you take control of the ball.

On the playing field of life, you can choose how to play. Sometimes, we just don't act like we hold our own future in our hands. It's easier at times to blame or justify why we have what we have. If you're spending any time at all fabricating excuses for poor performance, that's valuable time on the clock wasted. It's up to you to get the ball back and run with it. Successful people look within themselves to see how to create whatever outcomes they want. Taking responsibility means no more excuses, no more blaming, and no more justification.

The #1 Winning Point to accomplish your goals is to step up and be responsible for everything that happens in your life. That includes every single thing that happens in your life, good or bad, desired or not. *Everything*?! Yes.

Now let's take this concept even further because there are several levels of what it means to be "responsible." We've talked about how your thinking affects your performance. What I am now suggesting is that, in one way or another, your unconscious mind—those beliefs, values, and decisions you made a long time ago that you are no longer consciously aware of—is responsible for generating an even larger percentage of the results you get in life.

Thinking is a Team Effort

In order to fully appreciate how you are responsible for the results that you are getting, it is helpful to know how the mind works and how it influences your life. I recognize two parts of the mind--the conscious mind and the unconscious (or sub-conscious) mind. Did you know that 90-95% of your mind operates without your even being aware of it?! Only 5-10% of your mind is conscious! The unconscious mind represents realms of which we are unaware. When I ask you: "what did you have for breakfast this morning?" the answer is not in your conscious mind until you just read the question. Before then, it had already been stored in your unconscious mind as a memory, a picture of something that happened. That memory even has a feeling state or emotion connected to it—we will go into this more later.

While your unconscious mind is storing facts and experiential memories, it also files away the beliefs, values and other aspects of your personality you no longer think about consciously. You don't have to remind yourself every morning that you believe in being honest, right? That's because it's a value you developed a long time ago that you have probably long since stopped questioning.

Your unconscious mind is also amazing because it manages to store all the "how-to" manuals for most of the actions you perform throughout the day. In fact, most of what we do, day in and day out, we do unconsciously. Think about it...when you're tying your shoelaces, you don't have to consciously think, "Now I put the left lace over the right...pull both sides..." No, your conscious mind is thinking about the game or the meeting you're going to that day. It's your unconscious mind sending signals to the muscles that operate your hands so they get the job done right every time! Your unconscious mind also drives your bodily functions so you don't have to consciously think about digestion, breathing, blood circulation, beating your heart, etc.

Of course, the way training works is that, by repetitively performing the same action, it becomes integrated at the level of the unconscious mind and body. That's why we did drills as an athlete. Your coach had you practice a particular skill a hundred times in a row so that the successful completion of the motion became integrated into the unconscious mind. So you could "do it in your sleep" as they say.

You can, of course, make your every act conscious if you want, but why would you? Not having to think too much about your actions frees up your mind to think at a higher level - about strategy, creating or learning new things. The process serves us well for the most part.

The real problems arise when behaviors that are *ineffective*— that *don't* get us the results we want—become unconscious, and we no longer consciously understand why we're not achieving the goals we set for ourselves. Our own actions, decisions and emotions no longer seem within our control. We don't know where our behaviors are coming from. Our emotions are affecting our performance. The conscious mind continues to shout, *"Make more money!"* or *"Why aren't I advancing faster in my career?"* while the unconscious mind might be saying, *"You can't make money,"* or *"You don't have enough experience in this industry."*

You see how thinking is a team effort and your success relies on there being a positive, healthy relationship between your conscious mind—your captain—and your unconscious—your team. Remaining unaware of past decisions can hurt our game, on and off the sports field.

Your Conscious Mind As Team Captain

Think of your whole integrated mind as a sports team with a captain/coach and team members. Now, consider, who keeps the team on track—is it the captain, or the team members? The captain leads with direction and support, right? But, it's the team members who are doing all the work. They ultimately determine whether they achieve their goal or not, right? Actually, they need each other. Neither one can work well without the other. Your conscious mind is the captain, and your unconscious mind is the team members. They must work well together like a team and captain for you to get the results you want. There may be many conflicting points of view, but you are in charge of unifying the team and leading them to wins.

If you're shouting, *"I am a winner! I want to go all the way to the top!"* and somewhere in your unconscious mind, a voice is telling you, *"Well, it probably won't work out anyway. You know your father never really thought you were that good. Remember, it would mean so much to your mother if you'd just become a doctor…"* how motivated do you think you will be when it comes down to the finals? It's going to be much harder than it needs to be to hit your goals if you've got strong conflicting values working against you. This results in self-sabotage.

That's why it is so critical that the communication between the captain and the team members is perfectly clear. What is most important to success is that both parts of the mind are motivated towards the same goals and operating as one.

Your full power and strength to achieve anything comes from a clear mind, acting in harmony with itself.

Do you find that sometimes you sabotage, you prevent yourself somehow from getting what you really want? Do you repeat patterns of failure or never quite make it to the top?

Those patterns are indications that the conscious mind and the unconscious may not be in alignment. It can be very frustrating and for some, devastating to their career. When it starts to feel like you're self-sabotaging your own success, it's time to become conscious of what hidden factors are determining your results. That is exactly what you are about to do in this chapter's exercise—discover what's behind your wins and losses. Become consciously aware of what's operating at the unconscious level of your mind that may be affecting your ability to hit your goals on and off the court. Once you see them, you can choose to let them go and take full control of your life again.

No One Wins At The Blame Game
"When you blame others, you give up your power to change."
• Author Unknown

As your coach, I want you to recognize your true personal power. Step up and say, "I'm responsible for getting the results I want in my life." When you take responsibility, it means you regain control of achieving all that you want to achieve. Take responsibility for your current situation in life whatever it is. I want to clarify here, though, that when I say *you're responsible*, it doesn't mean it's *your fault*. I don't want you to start thinking, "Oh no, it's all my fault I didn't make it, it's my fault I didn't do this and that." This step in your training has nothing to do with blame or who is at fault. It's your *responsibility*, yes, but don't start blaming yourself. You want to avoid blaming, yourself and others in a way that robs you of your motivation and ability to change the circumstance.

For those of you new to this concept, it may be confronting to realize that you are actually *the cause* for all that has occurred in your life. It's important to look at this in an empowering way—this is really an exciting opportunity to access more power and focus than you even knew you had! Rather than transferring the blame to yourself and getting down about it, taking responsibility is about facing a challenge or setback head on, and asking good questions.

When you experience something you don't like, get in the habit of asking yourself the following questions:

1. *How did I create this?*
2. *What can I learn from this?*
3. *How can I get the results that I do want?*

The final question helps you to switch from focusing on the problem to focusing on the solution. This level of accountability will get you taking action in the direction you want. I personally like the "How" question because it is open-ended and gets the mind to search for answers. Too often people say, "I can't..." which is a statement that closes off communication. "How can I....." is a question that presupposes the possibility that I can!

Be Cause

When faced with an event you perceive as a "problem," instead of saying, "it's because of my teammate..." or "it's because the noise kept me up before the big game..." BE the cause. Imagine someone from the sideline cheering you on all day everyday: "BE the CAUSE! B-E the CAUSE!" That's your cheer and your mantra. Remember it.

By being the cause for your results, you avoid the wasted time and energy that goes into blaming something or someone else. You can avoid shaming other people and justifying your own part in it. Justifying is just another word for giving an excuse. I know because I was pretty good at it. I'd even justify the justification. Know anyone like that? To get the results that you want to get in life, you need to let go of the excuses. Yes, situations happen in life that seem to be out of your control; however, if you give your power to somebody else, or to some other factor, then how are you going to get where you want to go?

Some people ask, "What about the accident I had last year? I didn't make that happen!" "What about the coach not picking me for the team...that's not my fault!" I am saying in some shape or form, that it is your responsibility—you create your results by the actions you take or do not take, or perhaps by your thoughts and you can allow the experience to serve your growth at some higher level.

In any situation, there is a cause, and there is an effect. It's a universal force of nature. Are you the cause of your results? Or, are you the effect of circumstances around you? Do you make things happen or do things happen to you? It's like that classic line from Marlon Brando in the film "On the Waterfront," "I could have been a contender...." When you are focused on making excuses for why you are where you are, you are not taking responsibility. When you are living as an effect of circumstances, rather than the cause, you are living reactively and are helpless to change your results. You may come up with excuses for past and present results, perhaps blaming others, but does that ever help you get what you want? For example, "I'm late because of the traffic." Really, or did you just not leave in time to allow for traffic? Regardless, it detracts from what you can do *now* to improve your situation.

How We Create Obstacles or Winning Outcomes

It is not always obvious how you may have caused certain experiences in your life like accidents, misunderstandings, failures? I still choose to believe that I have created these misfortunes in my life. This attitude helps me to feel I've got a good grip on the ball. I can move forward and come up with solutions rather than feeling a victim of the whims of the world.

It is your habitual thinking, the emotions, and thoughts that will most often determine your outcomes. Unconscious fears, doubts, inner conflicts will sabotage your conscious desires. It's only when you start examining these, with brutal honesty, that you start to see the reason why events occur.

For example, as I will describe later, I came to expect little support from coaches in my volleyball career. My belief became, "I have to do it all on my own. I have to work hard to get any support." Interestingly enough, that's exactly what I got, or perceived I got. I was looking for all the proof, confirming evidence I thought I saw in others' acts and words that supported my expectation. Consequently, my experience was maybe tougher than it had to be. My inner obstacles created situations on the outside I had to overcome to play at the Olympics.

At any given moment, your brain is bombarded with information via all of your senses—feelings, sights, smells, sounds, tastes, kinesthetic touch sensations. In fact, it is reported that two million bits of information enter your senses at any single moment. Can you imagine if you had to be aware of all that information as it came in? You'd have a system overload. Imagine if you had to consciously think about moving your eyeballs to scan this page, or what if you couldn't block out everything in your peripheral vision while you read this particular sentence? Are you conscious of the pressure on your backside as you are sitting there? Do you feel the air passing into your lungs as you breathe?

You would go insane if you had to think about every single piece of input. In fact, the reason for some people's insanity is that they are not able to block out the massive amounts of data. Fortunately your mind has a processing system to manage the constant incoming information. In his book, *Flow*, Mihaly Csikszentmihalyi discusses how our body/mind filters down the two million bits of input to just 134 bits of information. That is a massive difference—two million bits reduced down to just 134 bits of information that the mind can think about consciously! The remainder is absorbed by the unconscious. The body/mind has a set of filters that determines what we pay attention to at any point in time. The way that it does it is to delete, distort, and generalize the input so that we can make sense of the information and manage it to conform to our current model of the world. Our internal filters that choose what to let in and what to filter out is set by our memories, our beliefs, our values, our attitudes, our decisions, and even our language. It must correspond in some way that is familiar so that the mind accepts that information, based on what it already believes is true. All of these will determine what you focus on. In this way, you get what you expect!

Since you cannot consciously process all that information, you do it unconsciously—what you experience then is always a reflection of what you are unconsciously looking at or sorting for.

What should concern you at the moment, as it pertains to your career and relationships, is:

What are you paying attention to and what might you be blocking out?

The easy way to answer this question is to look at what experiences you are getting. That will tell you a lot about the kinds of beliefs and decisions you have carried forward into your future, without conscious thought.

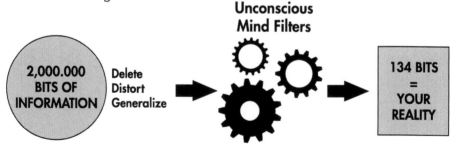

If you are seeing only 134 bits of information, you are only seeing the tiniest fraction of what is really happening out there. And these 134 bits of information at any single moment will determine your reality or your truth. This model explains why two people can have totally different views or perceptions about the exact same situation or event. I have had discussions with my sister, and we have completely different views on certain experiences in our childhood. I remember certain incidences very clearly, and she will have a different or less vivid experience of that same event. On the other hand, significant events in her experience passed through my filters unnoticed.

We tend to look for what we expect or want to see. What you perceive as reality will ultimately influence your results. Your past influences will determine what you see in life and likely create in your future.

This filtering down of information will also explain why some people see the negative side of things while others always see the positive. It is your "outlook" on life because you are looking out from the part of you that has already made up your mind about what it will choose to see. Think of your filters operating like the internet. The process of creating the results we get works like a search engine—every bit of information is out there but what you get back relies on what you put in as search criteria. So if you type in "life is hard," then you will bring up all the sites where life is hard. In reality, your 134 bits of experience, or your "results page," can only be comprised of data that supports what you already expect.

As a small example, I was chatting with someone who travels frequently, and he was telling me about his trip to New York and commented on how dirty the streets were and a few other negative aspects. He talked about another country and complained about the transport and the weather. I had to ask him, "so, what DID you like about New York?" He then became aware of other aspects of his trip that he had experienced but paid less attention to. The information was there but had been filtered out in favor of the negative experience.

You Get What You Expect

Have you ever said to yourself, "I knew that would happen!"? It's amazing our ability to be prophetic at times. Our expectations, whether conscious or unconscious, will often determine our results. Our mind communicates in pictures, sounds, feelings, and self-talk, and if you plant negative expectations into your unconscious, then that is the result you will get. Unfortunately, too much of our time is spent thinking about, and even searching for, the very things we *don't* want!

The trick to changing your results, then, is to change your expectations.

As an athlete, did you ever say, *"I don't want to fail!...I never want to lose another match!...I am not a loser!"?* Be careful—that is one way you might get exactly what you don't want because it becomes your whole focus. The mind doesn't hear/see/feel the "not." It only gets the pictures, sounds and feelings you create in your mind. If you imagine worst-case scenarios like not getting the job interview or your new business failing, what do you think you're more likely to create?

If what you perceive as your reality is a projection of what you are looking for, then this suggests that you can also be responsible for how you see your life and therefore the results you get.

By embracing this philosophy, you can now start creating better experiences in your life! Open yourself up to seeing life in alternative ways and you can be more attentive to opportunities that are out there...if you look for them.

It is not only our physical habits that produce the results. It is our habitual thinking that will most often determine our outcomes, including expectations based in the kinds of unconscious fears, doubts, inner conflicts that sabotage our conscious desires. It's only when you start examining these, truthfully, that you start to see the reason why events occur.

I think we create our own "luck" through our attitude, our beliefs as well as our actions. Many people have been touted as being an overnight success, but it takes years and years to become an overnight success, years and years of doing the little things that matter in the end. More often than not, it is the small ordinary things done regularly that earn us our success. That is why it can be difficult to see how we could have caused some of the situations we find ourselves in. Or perhaps you look at somebody else's results and consider them to be "lucky."

However, the little things done consistently can also create the undesired results in your life. Repeatedly eating the poor foods will lead to ill-health. Repeatedly trying to do the least can affect your results. Non-actions can be just as harmful. Not showing up for meetings, not learning new skills, not saying no—these all have bigger consequences in the end than we may ever recognize. Those insidious self-doubts or negative attitudes you tell yourself about your performance or abilities work in the same way.

When you catch yourself expecting negative outcomes, think about what it is you really want instead. For example, try this simple experiment next time you are running late for an appointment and stuck in traffic. Rather than reinforcing that you are going to be late, predict the time you will arrive (on-time) and create the picture in your mind of arriving on time easily. I've done this on numerous occasions and love how the traffic eases up or makes way for me, and I make it on the time I predict. You can use this to "predict" or anticipate many more useful results in your life.

You have probably heard of people who manifest parking spaces all the time. I do it with remarkable consistency. If that is possible, then what else can you manifest? What else can you create in your life? By applying the lessons of this book, you can have the ability to create whatever it is that makes you happy.

Here is an exercise that will increase your awareness of your thoughts and self-talk—what you are expecting and creating—so you can gain more dominion over your outcomes.

SUCCESS TRAINING EXERCISE:
What's Behind Your Wins & Losses?

• •

Think about some of the major events in your life to date and what decisions, expectations or actions you made that may have led to the result. What emotions were affecting your actions? How did your chosen responses to the circumstance affect your outcome? Some of them may have been good, others not so good. Take some time here to think about both and write them down in the two sections below—"Wins & Losses."

When writing down the reasons, be sure to write them down responsibly. That means, what did *you* do to have created the result in your life? Take your focus off of anyone else's part in creating the outcome, avoiding statements like, "so-and-so did this to me."

Your focus should always be where you have choice in the situation. Notice how your sense of power grows the more you realize the key role you play in the game of life!

WINS/ POSITIVE OUTCOMES

Result	**Be Cause**
e.g.) I made national team	I trained hard, I persisted, I enjoyed my sport.
e.g.) I have a great relationship	I listen, I communicate truthfully

LOSSES/ NEGATIVE OUTCOMES

Result

e.g.) I missed out on job

Be Cause

I didn't prepare for interview, I didn't really want it.

eg) I fought with my coach

I didn't listen, I thought I knew better.

_____   _____

_____   _____

_____   _____

_____   _____

_____   _____

_____   _____

_____   _____

_____   _____

_____   _____

Now that you understand that you have the power to create your results, it's time to consider the all-important question...*what is it you want to create??* And get excited! The great news is that when you have the master key—personal responsibility—you can unlock all the inner power and talent to perform at optimal levels in any arena and take control of your future. This is how a true champion thinks!

What do you want to achieve and who do you want to be? Start doing the things today that will produce the desired results tomorrow. Be the cause of your own success and destiny.

Summary

✓ Your repeated actions determine your results
✓ Your emotions and thoughts affect your decisions
✓ The meaning you give to experiences will ultimately determine your results

Ordinary things done consistently produce extraordinary results.

CHAPTER TWO

SET YOUR TARGETS

"You don't have to be a fantastic hero to do certain things to compete. You can be just an ordinary chap, sufficiently motivated to reach challenging goals."

• Edmund Hillary

Choosing My Future

I was only fifteen when I was advised that I could no longer compete in gymnastics. My dream of going to the Olympics was shattered. My initial reaction was devastation. My primary goal in life was to be a world class gymnast. Gymnastics had honed my discipline and had fuelled my ambition to succeed. Without it, I was lost and miserable.

Even at that young age, I was instinctively in the habit of finding other ways to reach my goals. I started asking myself questions like "If I can't do gymnastics, what other sport could I participate in? What sport would I possibly excel in? How can I still go to the Olympics?"

I was in of the 11th grade at high school and volleyball was something I played for fun. Some of my friends were playing in my early high school years, so I joined in, playing indoor volleyball with the school team. I didn't actually make the school team until the second year. One of my good friends was excelling at the sport, playing for southeast Brisbane, then Queensland. She was the one who really inspired me to try volleyball.

Other members of our school team also played in a Gold Coast club competition. Every year, our school team would dominate the competition, finishing on top at the end of the regular season; and then we consistently came unstuck in the finals and would finish second. It was so disappointing and frustrating to be so close but not go on to win. Then, in our last year, we finally learned our lesson. We pushed right through to the end and won the Grand Final. It was a really exciting victory for a team whose players had remained largely unchanged through the years. We had overcome our nerves and just went out there on the court to play the final like every other game, focused on winning.

My competitive edge started shining through when I was selected for our regional team, south-east Brisbane, where I experienced a different environment and style of training. Though our team won the silver medal at the State Championships, I was disappointed. I felt I couldn't rejoice in the result because I had sat on the bench during most of the games. Coming from the individual sport of gymnastics, I was yet to learn the importance of being a team player. That was a lesson I would learn later. Despite not personally seeing much court-time, I still managed to attract the attention of the state selectors and was chosen for the Queensland Under-18 squad.

In my final year of high school, I decided to select physiotherapy as my number one choice for a university degree. I had been introduced to physiotherapy as a result of my back injury, and I was drawn to the career as it would allow me to maintain my involvement in sport. My father was a chiropractor too, so I felt drawn to the healing profession. Interestingly, I didn't necessarily go into physiotherapy because I wanted to make people better. I was thinking that "here's another way I could get to the Olympic Games…if not as an athlete, then as a therapist." My dream remained alive and burning in my mind.

While studying physiotherapy at the University of Queensland, I continued to play indoor volleyball, establishing myself as a regular junior state representative. I didn't get much court-time at my first national championships in 1984 either. It was the start of my representative volleyball career though. From then on, I was consistently selected for Queensland junior volleyball teams.

The following year I found myself in the starting line-up, daring to hope that I might be selected into the Australian squad. At that stage, I didn't look ahead much further than the next competition and had no specific goals or direction within the sport. I had never even seen an international-level game and had no role models in the sport. I just always trained hard and aimed to be the best I could be. It was a "one step-at-a-time" approach. I wasn't chosen for the Australian squad after all and don't know if I even believed I was worthy of it. It's just that I was always striving for something, to be a better player, to get to the next step, to learn a new skill, and to keep moving forward in the evolution of the sport.

1985 was a great year for our Under-21 side. Our team won the national championships. It was memorable because we were a true team, with no huge stars of the time. South Australia and New South Wales had all the big names, yet Queensland defeated Western Australia in the final! South Australia was minus their number one player, Kerri-Ann Pottharst. Already one of the best players in the country by age twenty, she had decided not to play for some reason.

I had one more year in the Under-21 side, but we were unable to repeat the victory the next year. I remained "under the radar," unnoticed by the Australian selectors. My ambitions for a future in volleyball were still limited as I neared the completion of my physiotherapy degree in 1986. Since the national championships were coinciding with study week before final university exams, I was questioning whether I should play or not. I had studied regularly anyway and didn't feel the need to cram for the exams. I decided to go compete instead. My logic was that if I did not know my subject by now, I shouldn't pass anyway. Not only did I pass my exams, I also got to play in my final Australian Junior championship.

With my Bachelor in Physiotherapy degree in hand, and my university years of volleyball behind me, it was time to get a job… time to put those long years of study into a fulfilling career.

I applied to all the Brisbane hospitals for work, but no job offers came my way. I needed to look interstate for opportunities. On referral from two fellow graduates, I moved to Adelaide, South Australia, where there was a general hospital. There was a strong volleyball program in Adelaide that was supported by the South Australian Institute of Sport. I preferred this to the offer I had in Sydney. I quickly found a local team to play for and was noticed by state coaches, who asked me to join the state squad. I also travelled with the state Under-21 side, but this time as a physiotherapist. The coach of that team was to become the coach of an Australian Youth team, for which I was still eligible, and I was selected to play there too. Gradually, volleyball started to dominate my focus and my decisions again.

I had built a good rapport with the coach, Rob George, who taught me more than just the game. This is the point at which I began to learn about the importance of "character" and "team spirit," concepts I'd never really given much thought to during all my years of training. He'd drawn these principles from one of the most highly regarded coaches in the world, UCLA's well-known and respected basketball coach for forty years, John Wooden. When George introduced me to Wooden's "Pyramid of Success," which develops in depth all the virtues that create a champion, it was probably the first time I realized there was an inner-game going on that was just as important to winning as the physical game. I must have been a good student of the inner principles, as I was selected as team captain that year. We toured the United States, playing against colleges in the southwestern states, such as California, Arizona and Texas.

I took the principles to heart moving forward, practicing them just as I always did my skills on the court. I grew significantly in many ways and now recognize this period as a major turning point in my playing career, as well as my future off the court. One of the new skills I learned was goal setting. For the first time, I was encouraged to think about and write down my goals and to be clear about what I wanted to achieve.

For all my previous success in sport, and my previous dreams and aspirations, this was also the very first time that I truly started to think about where I wanted to go in relation to my volleyball and thinking of it as a career. Before that I had only approached it a step at a time...make the next team...win the next game. This worked for short-term goals, but it didn't necessarily weave into a long-term plan, and more importantly it made progress slow. In orienteering, you know only where the next clue is to be found. If you were to also know where the final destination was, it would speed up the whole journey. I didn't really know what my big picture was for my future, how far I wanted to go in volleyball, or anything else for that matter!

What did I want to achieve? I don't remember everything that I wrote down back then, but the ones I distinctly remember writing in 1987 were these:

1. Represent Australia at the senior level
2. Captain Australia

I set my sights on what was doable, and it turned out to be a good strategy. Though I still held onto my long-term goal of making it to the Olympics someday, I kept it real from day to day and continued to consistently accomplish my shorter-term goals...one play at a time.

• •

WINNING POINT #2:
Set Your Goals and Dreams High

"You have to set goals that are almost out of reach. If you set a goal that is attainable without much work or thought, you are stuck with something below your true talent and potential."

• Steve Garvey

The benefits of having goals cannot be overstated. Goals not only serve as major motivators on and off the field. They often become self-fulfilling prophecies. Here are some great examples:

- Once beach volleyball was announced as an Olympic sport in 1993, Natalie Cook, who had only just started playing and competing on the beach, set her dreams high—she wanted to win a Gold medal...she did in Sydney 2000.
- Greg Norman was just starting to play golf when he declared that he would win the British Open. This, in fact, was the only major he ever did win...he won it twice.
- Roger Federer set his sights on winning Wimbledon when he was fifteen years old. By the age of 21, he did just that.

Conversely, not having goals can leave you directionless. Without drive and a specific destination, you can end up going around in circles. In the story of *Alice in Wonderland*, Alice comes across the Cheshire Cat at a fork in the road. Alice asks the Cheshire Cat which road she should take. The cat replies, "That depends a good deal on where you want to go to." Since Alice doesn't know where she wants to go and tells the cat she doesn't care, the Cheshire Cat wisely responds, "Then it doesn't matter which way you go!"

What's Your End Game?

Many people are blindly going through life with no real focus, intention or purpose. I know some people who are even scared of writing goals down, for fear of being accountable to them, or fear of succeeding. I was that way after I finished playing volleyball, 100% focused on the court, and without any driving sense of purpose off the court, acting as if the same principles that worked in sport didn't apply to life. Some are happy to live their lives this way. They take whatever comes their way and that may work for them. But what if you are unhappy or unsatisfied with where you're ending up? What if you are missing out on living a full life or enjoying your dreams *only* because you didn't dare believe in your dreams? Or didn't want to admit to having any goals you wanted to achieve someday?

Some people have a vague idea of what they want but being too vague can lead to confusion and unwanted results. Imagine visiting a travel agent and telling her, "I just want to go on a holiday." And when she asks you, "Where specifically?" you reply, "Anywhere." The risk in that, of course, is that she may then book you to the next city a few hours away instead of the beautiful island, like Maui or maybe Tahiti, that you were secretly longing for. Or perhaps you wanted a snowy holiday, but you didn't have the nerve or the strength to say, "Yes! That's where I want to go." There's little benefit in keeping your secret aspirations a secret, especially from yourself! We all have dreams and desires. The first step to fulfilling them is bringing them to light.

If you are already an athlete, or have achieved other successes in life, you probably understand the importance of goal setting and have already done it on several occasions, either for yourself or your team. But are you applying the same attitude and process to your life after sport? What about your career?

A lot has been written and said about goal setting, yet there is still much to learn about how to precisely and effectively write down goals in such a way they are almost guaranteed to occur. In this chapter I want to show you the unique goal-setting process I use that can take your achievements to a whole other level—on and off the playing field.

You've got to set your targets before you can hit them.

Setting goals for yourself is one of the most important keys to getting where you want to go, and get what you want out of life. Instead of intermittent progress, stops and starts and getting stuck along the way, using this specific tool will keep you moving forward consistently toward the vision you old of your future. In the process, you get to learn what you are truly capable of!

Some people say that you should set your goals high in order to motivate yourself. Others like to set their goals low in order to feel the satisfaction of surpassing that mark. I believe the most important thing is not whether you set them high or low but that you really pay attention to what you want and what you believe about yourself.

My early volleyball career lacked focus *because* I lacked intention. I had never even seen an international game of volleyball in my first few years of playing for my state. I didn't know what to aspire to. Like a motorist driving in the night, I could see only as far as my headlights shone and taking it a step at a time did help me to get to a certain level. I did move forward, but it was pretty slow-going, and perhaps I missed some turns that could have gotten me to my destination quicker.

When I set a clear goal of playing in the Olympics, I achieved it. When I retired from playing in 2000, I had no clear goal or knowledge of what I wanted to do next. I was looking forward to settling down in one place and having a home. But I only had some vague ideas about what I would do in my career...sports marketing maybe? Media sounded fun. My biggest post-Olympics goal was actually to "just be normal." For me, that meant to settle down and get a regular job.

A regular job? There are a lot of those, and I didn't get any more specific than that for some time. Consequently, I moved around a lot from regular job to regular job. Some of these jobs were great – working with the Sport Institute in WA, the Olympic Council, and even a charity making a difference to kids from disadvantaged families. The problem was that they didn't hold long-term prospects for me and didn't seem to fit into a big picture or vision of what I wanted my life after sport to look like.

It took me six years to intently consider what my longer-term goals might be. After being so goal-oriented within sport, feeling directionless in life was especially challenging. I will discuss this phase I went through in a later chapter. As it pertains to goal setting, however, it wasn't until I finally started asking myself, "What do I really want?" that I made faster progress. I learned some specific ways to set and achieve life goals from a business mentor I then met. As a result, my life took off. I had direction, I had purpose, and I was motivated into action.

Some people go to seminars just to get psyched up with motivation. Well, that's like expecting that the pre-game session in the locker room is the only thing you need to win. That simulated sense of flying high only lasts so long; then unfortunately, those attendees come crashing down to earth again, too often ending up discouraged that nothing substantial has changed in their lives. But they didn't actually change anything about themselves or the way they've always done things!

Instead of starting high and ending low, this special process works because you start where you are now by setting realistic, reachable goals until pretty soon, your life is taking off to new heights. The sense of motivation comes from hitting each new target until you've built a track record of success and confidence. Larger career or life goals provide a powerful inner sense of purpose. It gives meaning and direction to the daily actions you must take toward it. The reason why so many struggle to get anywhere after sport is that they just haven't set a "somewhere" to get to. Without a goal, they lack focus and commitment to their future *and* their present.

Go For What Makes You Happy

When I have been most successful are the times I am focused on a goal, like getting to the Olympic Games. I've found most athletes are the same—without very specific goals, we feel a bit lost and directionless. It's critical that we develop goals outside sport that sufficiently motivate us.

Here's a big hint that will make this process easier and more effective—your goals should ignite your passion.

Now that I am focused on my business success, the sense of passion and purpose enables me to stay on my path, with a clear picture of where I am going. It's not necessarily a direct line, but I am always headed in the right direction, with slight alterations to keep me on course. Like driving down a long road to your intended goal, you are constantly adjusting the steering wheel, and there may be some detours or you may get stuck in the slow lane sometimes. As long as you stay on the road, you will eventually reach your destination.

So here is the special technique I use now on a regular basis to keep me and my career on course at all times.

The Dreams Process

The first step is to consider the big picture—where would you like to end up? Like Alice in Wonderland, if you don't know that, then you're not likely to arrive there. Remember the woman who let her travel agent choose her final destination point? Ask yourself, "Where do I want to eventually land?" Think about it:

*   *What makes you happy?*
*   *What do you want to have?*
*   *What will you be doing when you get there?*
*   *What do you secretly dream or wish could happen for you?*
*   *What is the ultimate big vision for your life?*

Take some time now to write down everything that comes to mind, short- and long-term goals. This is an important part of the process. Don't just ponder and daydream and say, "what if..." Dream big. And write it down!!!

Imagine...if you could really achieve whatever it is you want to achieve, what would that look like? Don't limit yourself by trying to figure out what is possible and what isn't. For now, don't think about how you're going to achieve it or whether it's realistic or not. Just put all your dreams down on paper (or your computer) so you have a record of them—this is the start to commitment and accountability to yourself and your future fulfillment of those dreams. Write it down like a wish list! This is where it all starts!

*   *What do you want to be?*
*   *What do you want to do?*

- *What do you want to have?*
- *Where do you want to travel?*
- *Where do you want to live?*
- *What kind of career would you love?*
- *What sort of net worth would you enjoy having?*
- *What kind of lifestyle?*
- *What kind of contribution would you like to make?*

Okay, now that you have a list of goals, it's time to take the next step. Just having goals doesn't mean you can or will achieve them...yet. I have found that creating a goal, using the following guidelines, enables me to strengthen my resolve and belief to achieve it. You can use this complete process on a day-to-day basis, particularly for upcoming events, training, or interviews, as well as for long-term goals.

Now you're going to take those big dreams and write them as reachable goals. This process of writing goals gives your unconscious mind clear instructions about what specifically you want and when you want it. Just remember this DREAMS Process for setting your goals:

D EADLINE

R EAL

E ND GAME

A T PRESENT

M EANINGFUL

S PECIFIC

1. Deadline

Set a deadline by which this goal must occur. You need to set a timeframe for your goal. Giving yourself a date by which you want it to happen provides greater definition and a greater sense of purpose to achieve that goal. If your goal is to lose five kilos, and you don't set a date then when will you ever accomplish that? Maybe never. Without a date you lose the impetus to do something right now towards achieving that goal.

You need to specifically state *when* you are going to achieve your goal. Though you may consider goals for tomorrow, or next week or next month, it is imperative that you specify the actual date by which you will be living that particular dream. If you write the words "tomorrow" or "next month," etc, then that is exactly where those goals remain...in the future. Tomorrow never comes!

Set a specific date, month and year. This is like setting a timer to go off, or knowing that the half-time game will be over in two minutes—you are more motivated to score within that given time frame. You know that whenever you have a deadline, it seems you always get the assignment done just on time, without a minute to spare. Well, if you had set the "absolute deadline" a week later or a week earlier, you probably would have also completed it just on time because there is the urgency to get it done.

Giving yourself a very specific timeframe not only gives you motivation, it gives you accountability. It is as if the conscious mind—your team captain—has given the unconscious mind the winning game plan. This gives your unconscious mind a sense of urgency to get things done and it will pull together whatever it must, however it can, to get the job done. Use this same strategy when you set your long and short-term goals.

2. Real

There's nothing more disheartening than when you share a dream or goal with someone and that person tells you to "get real." We also tell ourselves this same thing when we unconsciously believe something is not possible to achieve. Something inside may be telling you, "That's unrealistic. It will never happen." Then that becomes a self-fulfilling prophecy. In this case, when a goal seems out of reach, or unrealistic, it can stop you from ever even starting!

The key here is that a goal seems real to you. If you think a goal is beyond your reach, then you might not be motivated to do the work needed to reach it. As long as you believe in your goal, then it will inspire you to keep working towards it.

Whatever it means to be "realistic" is up to you—how do you feel when you think about that goal? We all have our own inner gauge; you don't need to heed what *others* claim is "realistic" or not. If the goal seems daunting and discouraging, then maybe it's just out of reach, and you can scale back on it a bit. On the other hand, if the goal motivates you, and you feel almost compelled towards going for it, then it's probably realistic. If you really believe and have the desire in your heart, you can achieve anything.

Only a very small group of friends truly believed that I could make it to the Olympics. As much as my family supported me, they were amazed and surprised when I actually qualified. I guess they had seen all my heartache, struggles, and setbacks to the point where it seemed crazy to think I could do it. I still remember my aunt's surprise when I told her I was on the team, and she said, "You mean you really made it!"

In the end, it didn't matter that my coaches didn't believe that I could do it, or even my family. It only mattered that I believed it. I felt it was within my reach, and that kept me moving forward through all those disappointments and years of training.

Setting realistic goals can also depend on your past success rate with achieving goals. You want to set the bar high enough that it makes you practice and play hard, yet not so high that it's discouraging. If you have rarely reached your goals, then it's better to start off with smaller goals. The actual achievement of goals, however small, can ignite a contagious sense of thrill and power that sets you off on a clear and winning path.

If you promise yourself to get up at six in the morning tomorrow and you do it. then you achieved your goal. It's that simple. Get on a success track by hitting one little target after another. You're racking up points with yourself. You're building self-confidence and determination that will translate in your performance. Give your unconscious mind, your hard-working team, a pat on the back and say, "Well done! Thank you. That's what I wanted to do. I've done it." Then move on to the next goal until you've hit that one too.

Achieving your goals in life is an ongoing practice, just as it is in sport. When you get really good at, it's time to stretch yourself. See what you can really do and accomplish.

Time is of the essence. Often people don't give enough time for goals to transpire. They think that they can achieve so much in just a few months or year. What might seem unrealistic may just need more time to allow opportunities to arise or actions to take effect. So when you're thinking ahead to your two-year goals, three years, five years time, I suggest you think big. Think bigger than you're currently thinking.

If you intend to set specific financial goals, and you aim to build your net worth to one million dollars in the next year, even if you fall a couple of hundred thousand dollars short, you could still be happy couldn't you? It's about aiming high! If you shoot for the stars, you can still reach the moon.

3. End Game

What's your end game? How will you know you have reached your goal? What has to happen for you to know that you have been successful? Is it when you have a certain dollar amount in your bank account? Is it when you are handed the keys of your new property or new car? This all depends on your goal. What are you striving for? By considering this measure of success, and the date of the goal, you will have very clear feedback on the results of your goal setting.

Get a Picture in Mind

Create your intended end game by imagining a snapshot in your mind of a specific moment in time—it will be the moment you realize that you have succeeded in accomplishing your goal.

For example, if you set a goal of earning a million dollars by the end of the year, rather than stating that your goal is to earn a million dollars, you are going to imagine the specific time you hit the million dollar mark. Can you visually imagine "$1,000,000" written on a cheque or bank statement with your name on it? Can you picture your accountant handing you your tax return and feeling totally excited to see that your net gain is $1,000,000? Perhaps the evidence is that you are looking at your bank account statement with "$1,000,000" jumping out at you. It will all depend on what inspires you the most.

Consider your next career goal. If you are striving to gain a certain position within a corporation or to start a company of your own, what will be the indication to you that you've arrived at that benchmark? For some it might be sitting behind a large cherrywood desk on their first day. For others, that one special moment might be when they sign the contract and think, "This is it! I'm in!" For you, maybe it's putting your new company logo up on the side of your office building and introducing yourself to your office mates, saying, "Hi, I'm Founder and CEO of..." whatever your new company is called.

Where's the Evidence?

Having specific evidence will tell you when you have reached your goal. This will also help you to acknowledge your achievement before going on to the next goal. I believe that high-achievers often feel that what they do is never enough. Some athletes are driven by a sense that they're not good enough, or haven't done enough, etc. I have often felt like this myself. This sense that all your hard work is never enough can lead to burn out. Then a good question to ask yourself is, "When is it good enough?" By monitoring your goals, both short term and long term, you can provide yourself with better insight into and perspective on all you really are achieving.

Over the years leading up to 2000, when I thought about my goal to reach the Olympics, the picture I often imagined in my mind was marching around the Olympic Stadium in the opening ceremony. That had been my personal evidence that I had reached my goal of making it to the Games, and served as a big part of my end game. Interestingly, that bit nearly never happened. In the lead up to the Olympic Games, as I mentioned in the Introduction, our coaches told us that we wouldn't be allowed to march in the opening ceremony, as we were to play the very next day. I was devastated.

The head coach's reasoning was that we were at the Olympics to compete and the opening ceremony would be a long and late night that could hinder our ability to play the very next day. Sarah and I felt very differently because we had had a fairly ordinary year of results, never finishing higher than 17, perhaps one 13. Looking at those results, we thought, "if we don't do the opening ceremony, it's just going to feel like any other competition, and we might end up producing that same result." Not only was I looking to the Olympic ceremony to build our energy, but it represented to me, rightly or wrongly, a huge part of what the Olympics were about. It was what I had dreamt of as a child, watching every Olympic Game since 1976!

We were given the opportunity to explain to the coaches why we thought we should be allowed to march in the opening ceremony. We believed that *because* of the opening ceremony we would play even better—that it would give us some extra drive and motivation.

The next step was to prove to the coaches that it wouldn't be a limiting factor. We did an experiment with the whole volleyball team and went out until past midnight to Darling Harbour, Sydney. Then we weren't allowed to go to bed until 1:00 or 2:00 in the morning, which would mimic how it would be during the opening ceremony. The fact that we were not staying at the Olympic Village meant that it would take an hour to drive back to Randwick, making the opening ceremony an extra late night for us.

After staying up late in our test run, we then had to train at ten o'clock the next morning. Sarah and I were pumped, and we trained really well. We trained so well, we beat our Australia number two team at that training. This demonstrated that we could handle staying up late and still turn up with the right motivation and be ready to play the next day. When we received the schedule for Day 1 and were given a 3 p.m. game time, it was decided that we could march in the Opening Ceremony after all.

Another of our Australian teams did miss out on marching, and I can't even imagine what my Olympic memory would have been like if I had not experienced that specific image that I had created in my mind years earlier that told me, "I made it to the Olympic Games! I accomplished what I set out to do!"

How will you measure your success?

Do you get a mental image of the moment you know you have achieved your goal? Consider where you will be and what you will be seeing, hearing and feeling that indicates you made it. Engage all your senses in the experience of that achievement. Then take a "snapshot" of that moment in time. With the next step, you will be able to fit the future moment in time into your present experience.

Michael Domeyko Rowland, in his book *Absolute Happiness,* provides another important distinction to consider. What's the complete picture? For example, you could determine receiving a particular income as proof of achieving a goal. However, this income could be cancelled out by a similar amount in expenses. The first year of my business I had a goal of $50,000 income. I achieved this but I forgot to specify *net* income i.e. after expenses, and that brought my business income to significantly less.

Rowland suggests that you consider the "proof of your goal achievement" as being even further along the time line. In this case, you could see the goal as being *net income after expenses,* or the goal could be represented by the lifestyle you are enjoying from that earning. Another example of a life goal would be to have a committed relationship with your soul mate. The "proof" of the End Game then might be the moment you meet your ideal partner and tell yourself, "This is it!" Or, if you went further along in time, you could imagine your wedding.

4. At Present

Here's the third criterion for this goal-setting process—state the future goals in the present tense, as if it's occurring now. Even though you have written a goal to happen at a future date, it is important to write the goal in the present. In quantum physics, time is just a construct of our mind and imagination, where there is really no future and no past, only now. When you picture an event, whether it is from your past, happening right now, or in your future, your unconscious mind cannot tell the difference. By writing a goal using the present tense, it enables you to step right into the goal like it is happening right now. The senses are immediate, so you feel, hear, and see it. This immediate experience of the future gives your unconscious mind the feeling that this goal is a foregone conclusion, and again, like the captain giving the team an order, the unconscious mind does whatever it must to achieve that end game. In my case, when I arrived at the Olympics, my future intention was so clear, I did whatever I had to, to make it a reality.

A goal to start your own company may sound like this: "I AM shaking hands at a networking function introducing myself as Founder and CEO of _____."

A goal to have one million dollars could read: "I am online looking at my financial statements, and I see I have one million dollars net worth."

Use present tense rather than future tense such as, "I will" or "I will be." Future tense tends to make that goal *stay* out in the future. In Australia we even have a term for these kinds of goals—"Gunna," slang for "going to," but forever put off. These goals usually remain a *someday in the future* goal.

Write it as if it's happening NOW "at present," by using "I am...," "I am doing..." or "I now have..."

Then insert your specific date in there. So, when you write the goal, you want to write it like it is now the day you've set the goal to occur. For example, "Today is August 23, 2010, and I am celebrating in my office with the seven other members of my team our first year in business!" Note that this presupposes the business having grown to seven employees.

5. Meaningful

A complete champion looks beyond him or herself to consider the effect of their goals on others. Do you think about the consequences of your goals? What impact will your goals have on you, others, the global community and even the planet? Do you have a win at all costs attitude? Or is it meaningful to you because it benefits more than just you? If your goal comes with the risk of harming others, then you might find that the achievement of the goal does not bring the rewards you were seeking.

If you reach your goal, what does that allow you to do? Making goals meaningful puts purpose and drive behind achieving them. Consider you want to reach a particular goal…what will it get you beyond the result itself?

If you want to have a top-of-the-line car or a wardrobe of designer clothes, consider why you want to have these things. Sometimes when I pose this question to myself, I realize that I don't really want the things as much as I thought. Those things may end up being a secondary benefit of having wealth or success, but consider what gives the goal meaning for you personally.

I believe that we are more likely to achieve goals and move forward in life by having a purpose and by being clear with that purpose. I am driven by the purpose to connect with people and to inspire others to make positive changes to their own lives. When we are living with purpose, then, I believe, somehow the universe conspires for our greater success, and opportunities come more easily. Keep that in mind when you're setting your ultimate goals, and even your daily goals—make them meaningful.

6. Specific

This final guideline is most important. Be very specific about what it is that you really want. My dream was to go the Olympic Games, and that's what I achieved. I didn't specify winning a medal or even winning a game! Muhammad Ali was renowned for his bragging pre-fights and would often recite poetry about his upcoming bouts. The amazing thing was, not only did he predict that he would win, but also which round he would win it—he was accurate in 17 of 21 poems!

Be specific and clear when you write your goal. Remember a team captain needs to be very clear when communicating with the team if they are going to work together for the same end result. If you have a financial goal and say, "I want to make more money," then be specific with how *much* more money. I could give you a dollar right now, and you would have more money, thus achieving your goal. But I'm pretty sure you would be disappointed, even though it was what you asked for. Be specific and put figures in it.

In the beginning it can be quite scary putting specific figures down on paper. The best thing you can do is to just start. Practice with some small figures. Achieve those goals and then build on them, continuing to be specific. If you want to travel, then where to specifically? Where do you want to go in life? In your career? Dare to dream! And write it all down.

State What You Want

Here's another important point: When you write it down, make sure you have stated it in the positive. Be clear about what you *want*, rather than stating what you *don't want*. It's surprising how many of us think more in terms of what we are trying to avoid! Someone may have a goal to reduce credit card debt and write the goal as, "I don't have debt" or "I don't owe x dollars." The problem with this is that our mind doesn't come up with images for negatives such as "don't" or "not." It communicates with pictures, sounds and feelings and the above statements just bring up pictures of more debt.

The unconscious mind will think it's getting instructions to remain in debt! You don't want it to create more debt, do you? So state it positively as, "I want a zero balance on all my credit cards and a million dollars sitting in my savings account." Being specific about what you want and being positive about it will help you work towards that, versus what you don't want.

So that's the DREAMS process for effective goal setting that will get you results more efficiently. A goal needs to have a deadline, it needs to be realistic, it needs to have an end game, it needs to be written as if it is happening right now, it needs to be meaningful and it needs to be specific.

Set Up The Shot

*"If you know what to do to reach your **goal,** it's not a big enough **goal**!"*
                                                    • Bob Proctor

Before you get started now writing down your goals in this next Success Training Exercise, I want to give you one more bit of information. We discussed the importance of goals being realistic enough to propel you towards them...but that doesn't mean, think small. Don't limit yourself to goals you currently know how to achieve. Imagine goals that *inspire* you to achieve.

Often, people will stop dreaming or writing down a goal because they cannot yet imagine *how* they could possibly reach it. The problem is that they are limiting themselves to their current resources and positioning. Their own mind gets in the way by questioning what is reasonable and possible. My experience is that, when you start by thinking about the *what* first, then the *how* will follow.

There is a part of your brain that we talked about earlier, called the "R.A.S.," which stands for your *Reticular Activating System.* Its function is to integrate those two million bits of information from the senses so it, in effect, acts like an internal radar system. It influences the level of consciousness, alertness, arousal, and motivation you have. When you set goals or have an intention, you are essentially "programming" your R.A.S. to look for what you want or need to fulfill your objective. You've directed it to keep a look-out and search for anything that will serve that objective. Your R.A.S. will bring your awareness to the opportunities or people that can help make it happen. Often these opportunities were already there, but you were not looking for them before you set the intention.

For example, if you decide to start a business, you will be actively seeking the information to help you get started. In addition, though, your unconscious mind will also be identifying opportunities for you, so you will suddenly notice the people you meet who can help, or you will come across a course of study that can improve your chance of success.

Before I went to my first fire-walking seminar, for example, I wasn't aware of how much information was out there in the way of personal development. Afterwards, I started seeing the multitude of courses and seminars available. A friend and I wondered whether they were only coming out now because personal development was becoming more popular. A closer look revealed that they had been around for years and even decades—I just wasn't out looking for them.

That's why writing down the goal is so critical to the process of attaining it—you've fixed your targets; now you want to keep your eye on the target while you start taking action toward it. The same thing will happen with your goals. When you write your goals using the DREAMS process, you will be directly communicating with your R.A.S. as to what is important to you. As a direct result, you will be alerted to opportunities, seeing the world with new eyes. What may have passed you by before previously unseen is now made apparent. Think of it like a *Where's Wally?* Book. You cannot see Wally in the pictures until you specifically seek him out.

I'm not saying that by following the DREAMS Process, you will achieve *each and every* goal you set. The important thing is, you've set up the shot. You may sometimes fall short of its completion. In sport, you might win a bronze instead of a gold. Or earn $800K instead of $1 million? Does that mean failure? Remember, you want to choose the attitude and meaning that best support your success.

When you don't achieve a goal, get the feedback from the result. Benefit from falling short of it by asking yourself, "What can I do differently next time? Where was I responsible for not reaching that goal?" In any case, the result you get is most often worth a lot more to you than if you hadn't set your goal so high! The result may spur you on to work harder, to keep going for that goal, adjusting the date for achievement.

The athlete who aims to *be* the best is better than the one who simply aims to *do their* best. This is as true in the playing field of life as it is on the sporting field.

By aiming high, your best gets even better. This applies to anybody and everybody and is the same on or off the sporting field.

The caveat with aiming high is that you need to be okay with failing. I was giving some coaching advice to someone disappointed with a 15-minute presentation she had just done. She berated herself for setting such high expectations of herself. I told her that setting high expectations was not the problem. The problem was judging herself a failure if she didn't attain it. This can lower your self-esteem and consequently lower your chances of going for it the next time. Each time you miss a goal or expectation, it's a chance to learn and grow. What did you do well? What can you do better? Daring to fail is the only way anyone succeeds. If you keep setting low expectations for yourself, then you might get the satisfaction of attaining your goals, but you risk playing a small game. Who are you not to play big?

For now, forget about the *how*. What kind of success would you like to achieve? Dare to dream big. Set your sights and go for the gold!

SUCCESS TRAINING EXERCISE:
Go for Gold

• •

All right, now it's time to fix your target! If you haven't already brainstormed all your big-picture dreams and visions for your future, do that now. Take the time to write down some of those goals using the following format:

Today is _____ (future date)_____ and I am/have _____

_____

_____

_____.

For example, *"Today is 10 August 2010, and I am in my house looking out over the beach, celebrating the news that my second book has shot up the ranks to number one best-seller."*

This goal already assumes I have the home on the beach and that I have written and published a second book.

Today is _____ (future date)_____ and I am/have _____

_____

_____

_____

Today is _____ (future date)_____ and I am/have _____

_____

_____

_____

Today is _____ (future date)_____ and I am/have _____
_____
_____
_____

Today is _____ (future date)_____ and I am/have _____
_____
_____
_____

Today is _____ (future date)_____ and I am/have _____
_____
_____
_____

Look back at your goals again and see whether you can stretch yourself a bit more. Can you go a little further outside of your comfort zone? You might not yet know how to get there, but at least by knowing where you want to go, you will find a way.

How much is that goal worth to you and what action will you take to achieve it? Are you committed? Will you persist? Decide what you want now and go for it! I will talk more about the game plan and working with your goals later in the book.

Summary
✓ Consider what you really want to achieve in your life
✓ Write down your goals keeping in mind the DREAMS criteria
✓ Be specific with numbers, amounts, dates, frequency, etc.

Be careful what you wish for....

CHAPTER THREE

PLAYER ASSESSMENT

"Believe and act as if it were impossible to fail."
• Charles F. Kettering

As I progressed in my sporting career, I had many influences over the years that not only shaped my early results; they also shaped who I became, personally and professionally.

I recently met up with one of my gymnastic coaches, and it was interesting to hear his viewpoint of my character and my potential when I was young, most notably that I stood out as someone to watch from a very early age. It got me wondering about what I must have believed about myself to set such high goals at such an early age and how I came to those beliefs. There was no history of sporting success in the family to inspire me. Yet, I always felt at some level that I was capable of doing great things. And I was very self-motivated from the start. My parents supported me, but they never pushed or directed me in any way. I had seen the classic "pushy parent" of some gymnasts, the ones who try to live their own dream through their kids. I was grateful to have grown up in a supportive environment, without the pressure. My parents were always willing to take me wherever I needed to go. My mother was actively involved with the gymnastic committees and shared every local competitive gymnastics routine that I performed, probably holding her breath. Dad was usually there too.

"I Am Special"

What was it that shaped my results and shaped my direction in life so early on?

In thinking about this question, I realized that I had grown up with a belief that I was special. I was special for two reasons, as far as I believed—I was born on a special day, the 1st of January, New Years Day. Every year my birthday was a special occasion that everybody in the whole world celebrated with me. This notion was constantly reinforced every time someone discovered my birth date and responded enthusiastically, as if my circumstance was totally unique. Over time, all their positive remarks about being born on such a special day translated as a belief in my mind that I too was then special.

Secondly, I was fortunate enough to be born the youngest of my siblings. Being the youngest child in a family is not necessarily a good position to be in, but I perceived it to be special. Perhaps it was because I was the last to go to school, and I enjoyed more time spent alone with my parents, especially with my mother, around the age of three to four. This nurtured a feeling of getting special attention at a very impressionable stage in my life. I would later strive to fulfill something special.

Even at primary school, when I was in grade five, I was put into an experimental class, where they combined the "smartest" kids from two grades. We were given different lessons than the regular students, I guess to see how that would influence our education. I was in that combined class for three years, and to this day I do not know the verdict of this co-teaching experiment.

What if we weren't even the smartest kids but were told that, to see how our grades would be influenced? I have gone through life thinking I'm pretty smart because I was chosen for that class. Was I smart before I was in this class or after I was given the label? I don't know!

It doesn't matter what the "experts" say or not; what matters is that I believed it.

Having those beliefs stirred in me a sense that I had unique attributes that allowed me to go further than anyone, that meant I could make it to the Olympics, that I was born a star. Even today I feel I have that special quality that enables me to do anything I set my heart and mind to. In fact, we all have that special gift. It takes the inner realization of that, however, to make it be true for you.

The fact that I fulfilled what I believed to be true is no coincidence. It demonstrates how powerful belief can be. I am very grateful for having taken that approach to life. Not everything I believed helped me though because not everything I believed was positive. I recognize that I also created challenges for myself by taking on negative beliefs, based on influences around me early on.

"I Have To Do It On My Own"

I was two and a half years younger than my sister, so I did grow up somewhat on my own sometimes. Spending a lot of time alone created a degree of independence within me. Throughout my life, I was quite strong, determined, and independent. This independence strengthened to a degree that it formed a belief in me that "I have to do everything on my own." Assuming that true, I projected that out into my reality and, consequently, that was exactly what I got. Unknowingly, I was creating situations that reinforced the necessity to do everything myself.

Because I felt the need to do things on my own, life situations became difficult. As I was growing up, during my gymnastics years, then into my volleyball career, I didn't ask for help enough, and it took me a long time to adapt to a team culture. That difficulty in turn created new beliefs like: "It has to be tough," and even, "It has to be tough to be worth it...anything easy isn't deserved."

"It's Not Fair!"

I'm not sure whether this belief was drummed in at an early age from my parents, but I do remember my father saying, "It's not fair!" At some point I took this on as my own sort of "mantra." He will probably hate me for sharing this, but when we played Monopoly, if he wasn't winning, out it would come: "It's not fair!"

There was one occasion in the summer of 1998 when I was playing a beach volleyball tournament in my hometown of the Gold Coast. It was a really windy tournament, and they had only recently brought in the rule that if the serve hits the net and goes over, the ball is still in play. The old rule was that the serve had to clear the net. We were playing in the final, and there was a series of points where the opposition had this curious string of luck—serve after serve, probably three or four in a row, hit the net and just dribbled over. They were unplayable. My partner, Sarah, and I, just had to accept it and prepare for the next point.

As this was playing, I got the thought in my head of my father, who was watching from the stands and probably not so familiar with this new serving rule. I imagined him saying, as yet another serve clipped the net and dribbled over, "Aw, that's not fair!" We did go on to win the game and claim the title. But, when I talked to my dad after the game, he brought up those freak serving points. I laughed as he commented to me, "That wasn't fair!"

I can see how this belief played a role in my life. I recall, even as early on as my gymnastic days when I would receive a score and it just didn't seem to be good enough, thinking that the system didn't seem to be fair. Often when I would receive a lower score than I expected, I felt cheated and would automatically play the victim role, thinking to myself, "That's not fair."

In the beginning, my gymnastics went really well, but as it got more competitive, and perhaps as that belief started to take shape,

I started to make situations more and more difficult for myself. Then I started to look outside of myself for reasons and excuses for why events would turn out the way they did. My parents supported my thinking, which only strengthened my existing belief that I had what it took but..."Why wasn't I getting the scores I deserved?" At one point, we even felt the judges were against me because of the coach that I had. Rather than looking within at my own ability, I decided to switch clubs to work with a new coach. I was looking for answers outside of myself to make thing fairer, so that the judges could support me, and my dreams.

Now I can see that, throughout my volleyball career, as my desire to be successful grew stronger, the limiting belief that, "I am not getting the support I deserve," and my conclusion that I therefore had to do it on my own, only got stronger. The two beliefs seemed to work hand in hand to create the truth I was experiencing. The stronger the desire to get what I deserved, the stronger that belief took hold, not consciously, but unconsciously sabotaging the outcomes I really wanted.

The belief was that it really had to be tough...and I certainly proved that true. I had to work twice as hard on the court to prove my point, because that was what I believed and was looking for. You remember how the R.A.S. operates? My Reticular Activating System seemed to only notice other players who didn't have to work as hard to make it on the court. Maybe they were more talented, I don't know, but it just seemed to be really hard for me. Everything I believed was proving true in my experience...as far as I could see.

What's True For You?

The model of the world we develop when we're young stays with us into adulthood. Even after we stop thinking about what we believe, it becomes implicit to who we are and the reality we create for ourselves. Unaware of how we're affecting what we get in life, we go on believing "that's just the way it is," even when that's not necessarily the case. Then, this old set of beliefs gets reinforced through experience as we continue to recreate the same experience over and over again. This is as true in business, relationships and health, as it is in sport.

At a certain point, I had to look at how my beliefs were affecting my finances. My understanding of money growing up was that the key to getting ahead was essentially, "Work hard, limit your spending and save what you can." This served me as pretty good advice that kept me safe and secure for awhile. I budgeted well and even had a system for dividing up my first source of income—my student support—so that I knew exactly how and where I could spend my money.

There is a fine line between being frugal and being miserly. I think I often crossed that line in the wrong direction. My education on finances was limited to saving. There is so much more to learn and practice when it comes to growing wealth. I now study successful entrepreneurs like Richard Branson, Warren Buffett, and Loral Langemeier to expand what's possible for me in business. I discovered that, from the time they were nine or ten years old, these future millionaires and billionaires were already thinking about how to make money through small business, such as lemonade stands and newspaper runs. I realized, I had never really thought about making money, only about saving what I got!

I managed well enough, having been instilled with this philosophy through the beliefs of my father. I always seemed to get by and have enough. The truth, though, was that I never seemed to get ahead either. Even though, like most people, I wanted to be rich, I never thoroughly considered how I was going to create my wealth. In fact, I didn't really believe that I could. I thought, "I'm just not good with money or finances." In fact, the few times I tried an idea like investing in shares or some multi-level marketing scheme, it would backfire and simply reinforce my belief that I had to work hard for my money.

It wasn't until I started reading more about business finance and learning the language of wealth that I started to break free of some old habits. I first read about creating income through property and, for the first time, I could see a point to buying a home. I could see that it was okay to have debt. I could see that money could work for me rather than the other way round. Why hadn't I been told this earlier? It didn't matter now. The important thing was that I knew it was time to write my own rule book for the game. I had been following other people's game plan long enough...now I wanted to play at my own game and win.

• •

WINNING POINT #3:
Believe It to See It

"Whether you believe you can, or believe that you can't, you are probably right."

• Henry Ford

Beliefs are an individual's way of looking at life. If you consider that there is no absolute reality, then it is your beliefs that determine your reality. They shape your world and determine the results you get in life, either directly or indirectly. So you best believe what best serves you and your success.

If you believe that "money is hard to come by," that will be your experience with money—it will be hard to come by. If you believe that "life is a party," then that will be the life you live. I've studied this concept, and I've seen the truth of this in my own life. I see how often we sell ourselves short on what we are capable of, or sell out on our dreams, just for the sake of staying true to our old beliefs. How do you "sell" yourself, not only to others, but more importantly, how do you sell YOU to yourself?

Without thinking too long about it, see what thoughts come to mind when you ask yourself:

- *What do I believe is true about myself?*
- *Do I believe I am capable of achieving my dreams?*
- *What do I think it will take to get there?*
- *Do I believe in going for those dreams?*
- *Or do I think that they are just that, dreams, and not something I can actually attain?*

Einstein said we are bound by the limits of our thinking, and that means we only know what we know until we search outside of ourselves. Outside of your model of the world, your version of reality, do you think you could come to realize that there is so much more? Think of your learning years and developmental years when you started to expand your understanding, didn't your world expand as you went from primary school to secondary school, and then from high school to university? With each stint you discovered there was more to life than you saw previously, and you became more aware of the possibilities open to you.

Your world expands along with your mind, opening up new potential for your future.

Beliefs play a major role in who we are, what we do, the actions we take, and the results that we get in life, in career, and in relationships. Your entire belief system was shaped early in life as you picked up beliefs from family members and peers. Those beliefs then acted as filters that helped you interpret your experiences, and lend them meaning, particularly early in life. When they became so accepted, they became your "truth," what you perceive to be true.

There are also "universal beliefs" that we all hold to be true, such as the sun rises in the east, or we need to breathe to live. These obviously shape our world and behaviors too. Then there are beliefs that we once believed and now no longer hold true. For example, did you once believe in Santa Claus? Did you once believe that carbohydrates were good and now you believe that they are bad? The latest research changes our beliefs all the time, often based on authors or scientists putting forward their own personal beliefs. Actually, none of this is "the truth." Even everything you are reading here in this book is a reflection of my belief system and is not necessarily true, right, or real.

I *choose* to believe these keys to creating success because when I do, they work for me. Since taking on new beliefs about the law of attraction, about being able to create change, I have been empowered to create greater success in my life and it can for you too. Choosing to get rid of a belief that doesn't serve you and incorporating a new belief instead that does support your success can affect positive changes in your reality.

Beliefs That Hinder Or Help

"Don't limit yourself. Many people limit themselves to what they think they can do. You can go as far as your mind lets you. What you believe, remember, you can achieve."

• **Mary Kay Ash**

Here's the important question to ask yourself about your beliefs: are they empowering you to get the results you want?

If they are not, then why not choose new beliefs that do help you get what you want? Perhaps you need a belief that will enable you to grow, a belief that you can be all that you can be, that you can achieve greatness in any area of life you choose. Choose the beliefs that empower you, and helps you towards where you want to go, over the beliefs that hold you back or limit your desire to take action on your goals. Not believing in your abilities, for example, stops you from going out to do the things you need to do to create results. That would be a limiting belief.

According to sociologist Dr. Morris Massey, from the time we are born to the age of seven, our mind and perceptive abilities act like a sponge, taking in every bit of information with no criticism or rejection of anything that comes our way. We each become so saturated in our own individual environments that the beliefs of our parents often become our own beliefs, almost without question.

Sometimes, we may notice that their beliefs don't serve them either because they are not happy, or they're not succeeding at anything, so we make a decision to have the opposite belief. But even this opposite belief has been influenced in reaction to our surroundings, and becomes unconscious so that we are not even aware that it's affecting our actions or inactions.

There are significant points in our development when we are making decisions that will rule the rest of our lives and shape the playing field they can play on. Here are just a few common beliefs that hinder progress based on early experience:

- *"I don't have what it takes to live the way I want to..."*
- *"It's hard to make money and I don't manage money well..."*
- *"You've got to work hard just to get by...."*

Entering the world of business then, if you approach this next phase of your life believing, "It's hard to get ahead," or "I have to sacrifice a lot to make any money," or "It's no fun trying to start a business," how do you think that will play out? In regards to my limiting belief that, "I have got to work hard to get anywhere," as soon as I realized I had the option to change it, I did. The difference it made in me, as well as my results, continues to have a ripple effect, positively affecting the way I do business and pursue my goals.

At the same time, I had this strong empowering belief about my ability to get to the Olympics. Perhaps it wasn't even so much self-belief as a strong desire and determination to get there. I made a decision to do whatever I could do to get there. However, I would not have driven myself if I didn't believe, at the unconscious level, that I had the ability to do it. So, what you believe about yourself is just as important to look at as what you believe about the world, or finances, or your future, or destiny.

My desire was strong, but there was also this doubt somewhere in my mind, "Can I really do it? I've got to do it all on my own." This made my path perhaps more difficult than it otherwise needed to be. I constantly had to deal with a lack of support from coaches, or so I perceived. Looking back now, however, I see that there were plenty of times when I was supported, there were plenty of people who believed in me and or tried to support me, but I was looking to the wrong people, to the wrong events, or choosing to hear the wrong words. Rather than feeling supported, I continued to push against, generate resistance, and make it harder for myself. If only I had asked for help, if only I had listened to those supportive words, how would my career have turned out?

Now I constantly look at what I believe about any given situation. I ask myself:

"What have I decided about this situation that is creating difficulties?"

Because, life is meant to be easy, it really is. When you start believing that it's designed to work well, you start seeing the easy opportunities that are out there.

What Shapes Your World?

Muhammad Ali had a very strong self-belief—he considered himself to be "the greatest." He repeated this over and over again with obvious conviction. How empowering would that be for someone going into a boxing ring or any competitive match? Ali also had a strong belief in helping others and being a good role model. When he was young Ali was excited about seeing his idol, Sugar Ray Robinson, and waited eagerly for him to get an autograph. When Robinson snubbed him Ali decided that he wouldn't let the disappointment get the best of him. He also decided that he would always have time to give autographs. We all have significant times in our lives when we make a pivotal decision, and perhaps it becomes a turning point in our lives. What we decide can determine whether we go on to succeed or follow a different path. Remember, you can succeed because of your challenges or you can fail because of your challenges. You decide.

Roger Federer used to have quite a temper when he played tennis, often throwing his racket down on the court. A turning point came after a tournament in Hamburg in 2001 when Federer decided that he needed on-court composure to make more effective use of his talent. It was a bit of trial and error to find the most suitable on court temperament, but it eventually became the strength of his game. Now he is considered one of history's greatest and gracious tennis players.

Your Search Engine

Consider your mind to be like a search engine for the World Wide Web. The input into your personal search engine is what you are looking for at any point in time. If you have a belief that "Life is unfair" and you put that into your search engine, what is going to come up?...all the situations that show you that life is unfair. Humans look for validation of their beliefs. You get what you look for.

Think about someone who annoys you—do you tend to notice and focus on the annoying habits of that person rather than their more desirable traits? If you believe that you are "no good at anything" you will focus on all the proof that you are no good and ignore all the times that you do well, even if these times outnumber the bad! Any proof to the contrary becomes an aberration, an exception that you essentially ignore.

What beliefs are you putting into your search engine? Do you like what you're getting as result? Just because a belief works well for someone else doesn't mean it will help you too.

My beach volleyball partner, Sarah and I had an interesting difference in our preparation for tournaments. She believed that she needed to go out and get in touch with the ball in the morning of competition and get some rhythm. This meant being out on the court between six and seven o'clock in the morning. Well, that was great for her, but I had a belief that I needed sleep. For the good of the team, I would go down to the courts with her that early, but begrudgingly. Getting what Sarah needed benefited us because she did play well. What often ended up happening though was that teams would then serve me, and because I wasn't doing what I believed was right for me, I ended up playing poorly.

When I realized that the early morning sessions were not working for me and that it wasn't best for the team after all, we worked out a win-win situation. Sarah would go down early in the morning with the coach and get that touch on the ball while I would get my sleep. We would both have the optimal preparation for our game because we each were acting in alignment with our separate belief systems.

During my Post-Olympic career, I bought into the belief that my profile wasn't high enough to succeed in media. As you can now imagine, this, of course, proved true. I assumed that you had to be one of the few really high-profile athletes to succeed in media. So I found myself noticing only the high-profile athletes succeeding in media and barely noticed other athletes who had not had high-profile careers, successfully enjoying a career in media through their own talent, persistence, and self-belief. The problem with many beliefs is that you can always argue strongly for them and say quite convincingly (for yourself and others) that it is true, that that is the way it is. You can even produce evidence!

"When we argue for our limitations, we get to keep them."

• Evelyn Waugh

Some people believe you need to have special or certain attributes to create particular results. You may know someone that believes "it takes money to make money." Believing this will stop someone without money doing anything to improve their financial status as they unconsciously perpetuate their dire financial circumstance to support that belief. Rather than study the successful business owners who rose up from poverty and made their wealth by being resourceful, that individual will corroborate their limited perspective by noting only rich people who make their money from having money. The reality is though, if you were to really stop and look at the situation, you could probably produce just as much evidence on the other side.

To start getting the results you desire in life, you need to have a look at the belief patterns that have shaped your life and are currently still influencing what you think and do. Your current results will be a reflection of your beliefs and the decisions you have made previously.

The first step in making any changes is *awareness*. Start to think about what beliefs you played out in sport that you may be holding onto as you transition into your next career. It is said that how you do one thing is how you do everything. Wherever you have pain in your life, you are likely to have a disempowering belief pattern. By the same token, your ability to create success in sport can carry over to creating success in other areas when you believe you can. Whatever you believed about yourself in sport is likely to influence your self-esteem in general. It's time to get brutally honest and dig deep because when you do, the climb up the other side is so much easier.

SUCCESS TRAINING EXERCISE:
Measure your Game

. . . .

Here are two methods for gaining insight into your unconscious beliefs. A personal life coach might use either method to get at deeper core issues.

1. Write down all the beliefs you have that may be holding you back in the areas of success, business, money, health, relationships, etc. Ask yourself:

*   *What do I believe about my ability to succeed beyond sport?*
*   *What do I believe about money and finances?*
*   *What do I believe about my worthiness to have what I want?*
*   *What do I tell myself and others about the world? Sport? Business? Myself?*

Or consider a problem in your life and then ask yourself:

*   *"What must I believe about 'x' to be having this problem?"* e.g.) "I can never get ahead. I always have to try harder than anyone else."

_____

_____

_____

_____

_____

_____

_____

_____

_____

_____

_____

_____

2. Look at some athletes/businessmen and women who have achieved the kinds of you successes you would like to achieve. What are some beliefs *they* held that led them to where they are now? If you don't know, you can guess based on their results or study them as role models.

_____

_____

_____

_____

_____

_____

_____

_____

_____

_____

_____

_____

_____

_____

_____

3. To prepare to play your best game, it's essential now that you replace those beliefs that no longer serve you with beliefs that support you and inspire you forward. It's time to choose new empowering beliefs. You can simply adopt a belief that is more suitable and more results-driven. You may even write down your belief as an affirmation and repeat it on a daily basis until it becomes part of your new belief system. What empowering beliefs would you like to have? What beliefs would best serve your goals?

_____

_____

_____

_____

_____

_____

_____

_____

_____

_____

_____

_____

_____

_____

_____

_____

Belief Busting

Sometimes the awareness of your limiting belief alone will be enough to drive you towards a new empowering belief, and towards more effective action. This can be hard, however, when part of you is in denial or resisting the new belief. It might seem familiar to you to say, "Money comes easily to me now" while your inner voice screams, "Yeah, right! Prove it." It can be very difficult to reprogram old thinking patterns by simply affirming a new belief when part of you is sabotaging the attempt. If this is the case, there might be deeper-seated beliefs you're not aware of consciously.

It is then more effective to go back, either consciously or unconsciously, to the stored memory of that stage of life when you first decided to have that belief. This could be a significant time in your life when something happened to cause you to believe something was undeniably true. For example, if you saw your mother and father fighting constantly as you were growing up, you may have decided that "marriage doesn't work."

In this case, you could go back in time in your imagination and remember specifically when you first decided that was true. Often this is difficult, and it is easier to do with somebody else under hypnotic trance, to explore the past unconsciously. This is especially useful if the past experience was traumatic or highly emotional.

So the addendum to this Success Training Exercise is that, if you're having challenges letting go and replacing an old belief, you need to get the lesson from it that will allow you to move on. The most important part of this process of unearthing old beliefs is to LEARN from the event. I believe that all events happen in life in order to help us grow and develop strongly. When we get empowering lessons from these decision points, we can then go on to lead our lives in empowering ways. When you see all challenges as a gift rather than a travesty, then you can be more pro-active in learning now, and carrying new more positive beliefs into the future.

When you go back to a past event, it is important to watch it from afar, like a third-party bystander so that you can learn what you need to from the past, without getting emotionally caught up in the disempowering memory. This technique enables you to get a whole different view of that particular situation in the past, while maintaining an emotional distance and empowered vantage point.

For the purpose of gaining strength and power to succeed, ask yourself the question:

- *"What is there to learn for myself that will enable me to move forward in life?"*

You Need to *Want* to Change

However you work to change your beliefs—through affirmations, through hypnotic trance, with a coach or without—it is vital that you want to change. If part of you either fears the change or feels there is benefit to keeping the limiting belief, then you will not change. Some people, for example, find it convenient to have a limiting belief as it stops them from having to make any effort to move forward, or keeping the old belief system in place saves them from having to try and possibly fail. It allows them to be lazy or, for others, it allows them to avoid disappointment or "save face." The fact that you can't fail if you don't try is comforting for some. The problem is that you also cannot succeed if you don't try. The more you fail the more you will succeed, and when you start to look at the possibilities of what you can do, the desire to change will become greater.

Summary

✓ Beliefs are shaped at a very young age
✓ Your beliefs determine your results and how you see the world
✓ Beliefs either empower you or hold you back

It's not our experiences that shape our lives; it's how we interpret those experiences.

CHAPTER FOUR

THE UNWRITTEN RULES

OF THE GAME

"You have to learn the rules of the game. And then you have to play better than anyone else."

• Albert Einstein

Doing It My Way

Throughout my life I have been committed to excelling in everything I do. From the age of seven, sport was an important part of my life. Given the chance, I would almost always choose sport over other activities, including social gatherings or holidays. This included a commitment to my health, fitness, and time management to make success possible. In volleyball I prided myself on my dedication to fitness and always pushed hard to be the best. These were the areas I valued most, and therefore expended the most time and effort.

Though it's easy to assume that others share our same values, they often don't. Differing values can be a potential source of conflict between teammates, colleagues, friends, family members, cultures, and countries. Exploring your own values is a great opportunity to become aware of what is truly important to you and what is not. This self-assessment can serve you in the same way as fitness testing helps athletes to demonstrate their strengths and discover what weaknesses they need to work on.

In the late eighties and early nineties, the indoor volleyball national team came together for training camps once or twice a year, prior to major competitions. We always started the camp with a fitness test and would exert so much effort during these tests that we invariably trained the rest of the week with severe muscle soreness.

I was such a fitness-nut with a desire to put 100% into it that I would really push myself hard, even in the testing phase. Once, at training camp in Canberra, I recall a fellow player telling me to slow down. I was either making them look bad or making them work much harder than they really wanted to. The comment made me stop to think, 'Why *did* I push so hard in a test?' Did it really matter what my result was? I realized how important it was to me to give everything my best while most of the other players seemed to have a different outlook on the fitness testing process—they were more concerned about surviving the week without muscle soreness.

This was a great opportunity to re-examine the way I approached sport. Reflecting on it now, I recognize that I highly valued hard-work, as well as honesty and giving everything my all, whether it was a competition or not. In the end, I was grateful that I pushed myself because it was that attitude that kept me in national teams and, ultimately, created my success in beach volleyball, a largely self-driven sport.

Health Vs. Weight Goal

Meanwhile, I also valued my health, having grown up with natural foods and remedies thanks to Dad being a naturopath. Due to my upbringing, being fit and healthy was an integral part of who I was. I didn't have to think about it much. I couldn't imagine trying to succeed in sport without being fit. I even had extra incentive to be fit because I was considered short for volleyball. I needed to be able to jump higher, be more explosive and have the endurance to compete against the taller athletes. I ate well and considered food as fuel for my body, as opposed to a treat to indulge in. This influenced the way I ate—very efficiently, always keeping in mind how it would affect my energy and performance.

At a certain point in my teens and twenties, however, how I looked in my bikini also became very important to me. How I looked began to unconsciously "outweigh" health as a priority. Keep in mind what I mentioned about people having different values systems. Well, sometimes our own values can come into conflict with each other in our own mind. This can be very confusing and generate habits that don't serve our higher goals.

I am about to share with you something I have only told a few people in my life. What's inspired me to tell you my secret is that I was at a network lunch the other day where we were all encouraged to "get real" and disclose something a little more personal about ourselves. I dared to stand up and reveal what I was doing behind closed doors at one time in my life. The perspective I got from looking at the reality of my confusion helped me realize that my confession belonged in this book so that others could learn from my mistakes. Originally I had not thought of this phase of my life being in line with the theme of success for this book, but I saw how important it is that we each acknowledge our pasts. It helps us to see more clearly how far we've come, so we can move forward more powerfully and effectively.

When I left gymnastics at sixteen and moved out of home to go to university, I started to put on weight. This was quite natural for that age, but after being so athletic and slim, I rejected my developing curves. It wasn't until I was in my last year of university that I started to seriously diet and was conscious of every bite I took, weighing myself daily. I also walked as much as I could and continued to train for volleyball, so by the time I graduated from Physiotherapy, I was consistently 54kg and felt pretty good about my figure. Looking back at those photos now, I can see how skinny I was. I rejected any suggestion that I had a problem as I felt I was still eating healthily, though sparingly.

When I moved even farther away from home, getting my first job in Adelaide, I started to break from my strict diet, and the weight started to come back on. I was still slim, but I didn't see it. One night I went out with friends and ate what I thought was too much pizza. I felt sick and hated myself for not having the discipline to say no. That night I became a bulimic. I made myself throw up so that I would not have to digest the pizza. It started off sparingly, and I didn't purposely set out to overeat, but it became a lifeline for me, just in case I splurged. I saw it as a bit of freedom after years of strict dieting. I didn't feel free within my mind though.

When I went to The Netherlands to play professional volleyball, the unhealthy habit intensified. Often bored and left to my own devices, when I wasn't playing or working, I would just eat whatever I could find, knowing that I could throw it up. Generally, the times when I was at my unhappiest was when the bulimia would become more apparent. For fifteen years it was part of my weight management system...all so that I could look good in a bikini! Ironically, when it was at its worst, I weighed my heaviest. Not a very effective system.

It was also my secret. I didn't tell anyone, and no one ever suspected. I'm sure my friends reading this will be shocked, but I was too ashamed at the time to say anything, and I didn't want anyone to try to stop me. If people knew, I probably would have felt guiltier with each unhealthy act.

Before my mother died, I did share the secret with her. I also told my brother and sister but no one else. When I decided that I wanted to be healthier and happier, I put bulimia behind me. I consciously chose to not do that anymore. Even now on the occasion when I've eaten more than usual, that old thought might arise that I can get rid of it. That's when I remind myself, "I'm a healthy eater now."

The choices we make are always based on what's important to us at the time.

Reflecting on my behavior at that age, I can see the habit came from believing that "looking good" was more important than taking complete care of my body. Now I consider the importance of my health, my teeth, and also my character. I don't want to do anything that would make me feel ashamed. Not only do I have a healthier body image, I have a healthier self-esteem. Health being a high priority value once again dictates that my eating habits remain consistent with that value.

Setting Priorities

Here's another example of another potential conflict between competing values. Numerous times throughout my career as a professional athlete, I had to choose between a sporting commitment and a social gathering. At high school, while all my friends were going to parties and under-age discos, I was training for gymnastics. Even at university, where partying can be a priority, I continued to limit my socializing to make volleyball a bigger part of my life. I did go out, and I did enjoy parties, but it was considerably less than most people in their late teens and early twenties. I'm sure most athletes can relate. It's a choice we often have to make.

The choice was harder when family commitments arose, and sometimes I would have to choose my sport over them. I was so focused and committed that invariably I went with the sport, whether it was training or a competition.

The choices I made all came down to what was important to me. Playing sport stayed at number one value. That was why in my last year of physiotherapy studies, I chose to go and play in the national competition in the study week prior to my final exams. It wasn't that my study and my career wasn't important to me, but less so. Fortunately, I had studied well enough throughout the year to feel confident of passing. The choices I made along the way reflect the results I got—I continued to climb in my sport career. I was also fortunate to have a supportive family that respected my decisions and understood when I couldn't be there with the family. I was still able to maintain healthy family relationships.

My other relationships suffered more. I see now it was only because I didn't make them a priority. It was easier to maintain friendships within my sport because not only did we share the same interests, we were already spending so much time together. I have very few friends now from my school or university who were not also involved in volleyball. Those I keep dear to me are the ones who appreciate the time we do have together and the contact we might have through phone calls, emails, and now Facebook.

Though values are often reflected in how we spend our time, I have one friend, Leesa, I've known since early gymnastic years when we were twelve or thirteen. Though we live in the same town of Queensland, on the Gold Coast, we see each other only every six months, as result of all my travels and our various commitments. Despite this, I still consider Leesa one of my closest and dearest friends, and I know that she is there to support me in anything I do. Each time we do see each other, we just pick up where we left off, and fill in all the blanks.

My personal relationships suffered even more, however, as I never seemed to make the time for a boyfriend. Even though I wanted one to share my life with, in my earlier years, my sport would almost always come first. I lost one of my first true loves because he felt he wasn't as important as my volleyball. I was devastated because I didn't feel that way, but I guess my actions were telling a different story. We were at different stages in our lives and at 23 years old, I had more volleyball to be played.

• •

WINNING POINT #4:
Value Yourself

"When your values are clear to you, making decisions becomes easier."
• Roy E. Disney

We all possess a unique set of values that acts as a sort of rule book for living, that guides the choices we make, how we spend our time, where we invest our wealth, etc. Tony Robbins considers values "like a compass that directs your life." Our choices and behaviors are ruled by those top values. Whether individuals get what they want or not can often come down to their priorities, what their existing values system dictates.

Do you know what values you live your life by? It is likely that you picked up your current values from those around you growing up. You won't do anything that falls out of your value system, even though you might not be aware what they are. More importantly, it is your top five values that determine your life and the results you get. Values can have a significant impact on the results you are currently getting and the results your desire. So it's time to figure out:

* *Whose rules have you been playing by that have determined your results up until now? and,*
* *What rules do you want to play by moving forward?*

Whose Rules Are You Playing By?

A value is simply what is important to you in life or various aspects of life. Values tend to be words or phrases like "love," "honesty," "fame," "financial security," "living life to the fullest," "playing

100%" etc. You can have a separate set of values operating within the area of career compared with your relationship values or your broader life values.

The problem for me in my post-volleyball years was that I was still living my life by the same "rule book" I had previous to retiring from sport. It had served me during my sporting career, but it wasn't what I needed to help me move forward into business or relationship or family, etc. When I first learned about the impact of values I took an in-depth look at what was in my personal rule book and how it had dictated some of my decisions and behaviors. I saw that "independence" had been at the top of my list for a very long time. I also valued hard work, integrity, and teamwork.

Money, however, in the form of financial reward was far down on the list in terms of my priorities, which was evident in the results I was getting at the time…or wasn't getting. And "love" didn't even appear on the list at all as far as I remember!

So, if values determine results, compare the following two values systems and consider the results each person might be actually getting in their lives:

PERSON A

Hard Work #1

Family #2

Health #3

Helping others #4

Variety #5

Honesty #6

Financial security #7

PERSON B

Financial Reward #1

Lifestyle #2

Adventure #3

Growth #4

Contribution #5

Travel #6

Family #7

Person A is likely working harder than Person B because "hard work" is what he or she values, whereas Person B may be spending more time investing in lifestyle activities, like boating or traveling.

Person A is also not necessarily being financially rewarded for all his or her hard work. In fact, Person B is more likely to have more wealth and more time to enjoy it, because his top two values are Wealth and Lifestyle. Person A's experience may be just as fulfilling through spending his or her time doing family activities, because he or she prizes "family." I show you this to demonstrate that—we experience what we deeply value.

Internal struggle and a sense of lack of fulfillment, meanwhile, often arises when what we *want* to get, or what we *say* we value, does not match up with what we're actually getting.

Someone may *say* "success" is important to them when really there is a deeper held value like "security" determining their decisions. They may choose to stay in a secure job rather than going for personal success goals. How could that be? Because most of us just "downloaded" our values system a long time ago from those closest to us, than stored it away in the unconscious and forgot about it.

Choose Your Role Models Well

Role modeling is a natural process done unconsciously from the moment you were born. We learn everything—walking, talking, dressing and driving—by observing and doing what others did, usually our parents. Even our values and beliefs are developed through modeling those closest to us in our most impressionable years. According to well-known sociologist Dr. Morris Massey, values are developed through three significant periods in life:

0 - 7 years of age
In the first seven years of a child's life, that child absorbs information like a sponge, accepting much of what they see and hear as true. Influences come from family, friends, religion, culture, geography, economics and the media. This is the period of time when a

child is told directly or interprets what is "right and wrong," "good and bad."

7-14 years of age

From the ages of 7 to 14, children start to look outside their family for role models. It is said to be the time that they look to their "heroes" and are influenced by others' values and attitudes, whether it's a teacher or a comic book hero. At this age, the child has learned to accept or reject ideas, filters them so to speak, based on how they fit in with their previous experiences.

Dr. Massey has noticed that it's the heroes we have at age 10 who have the biggest influence on who an individual will become.

14 – 21 years of age

Between 14 and 21, we are very largely influenced by our peers. Individuals are in the process of developing their outward personality, integrating values and belief systems, forming a way of seeing the world based on everything they've absorbed or rejected. Other influences of media, family, friends, geography, culture, religion continue to have an effect on their sense of identity.

Significant emotional events in an individual's life will also influence them. Abuse, achievement, trauma, etc., can alter someone's values and belief system. The experiences can shape their perspective of themselves, of others, and their worldview. Whether it's a positive or negative emotional event, a one-time incident, or occurring over a period of time with repetition, it contributes in some way to the unique "rules of the game" that individual creates.

During the long process of personal development through modeling, an individual's values and beliefs create their version of the world and their reality. This means their Reticular Activating System is constantly looking for evidence to confirm the same values and beliefs they already hold true, and reject anything else that doesn't fit into their model of the world.

This is how you can become boxed in by your thinking over time or… create champion values that last a lifetime.

In thinking back to how I formed some of my values, I realized that Nadia Comeneci had been more of an influence than I realized. Her success not only ignited my own Olympic dream, I had also assimilated a very similar eastern philosophy type of value system during my sporting career, particularly in the early years—I was tough on myself, disciplined almost to a fault, pushing myself to the limit, and denying myself tasty and tempting foods. It's interesting to note that, even Nadia admitted years later to struggling with anorexia and bulimia.

I was very independent and prided myself on the fact I could say, "I did it myself!" It was only within this past year, in fact, that I took a closer look at whether this extreme independence really best served my true needs and desires. That's when I realized it was not as positive a force in my life as I had thought it was in some ways. Upon closer examination, I saw that my independence was actually driven by a lack of trust and desire not to be dependent on anyone. I was motivated away from what I didn't want—a sense of dependence—rather than motivated towards all the benefits of independence. This is not a very effective way to be motivated. It gave me the inconsistent results I was getting, probably contributing to all my stops and starts.

Once I was aware of this less effectual dynamic going on within me, I chose to completely reprioritize my values. Independence was no longer important to me. I was able to see that there were always many people around to support me if I had allowed them to. Now I can appreciate the benefit of asking people for help and enjoy working together for a common goal. Fear of dependence is out of the picture completely. Because of that, I now place a very high value on relationships in my business and in everything I do, which makes reaching my goals a whole lot easier.

Champion Values

"Until you value yourself, you will not value your time. Until you value your time, you will not do anything with it."

• M. Scott Peck

One of the most important reasons I see values as being critical to a person's results is that it also determines a person's character. A complete champion is a champion off the sporting field as well as on it.

In researching what it is that makes some of the world's best known and best loved champions, I looked into what values systems they held as they were growing up and as they were succeeding on the world stage. By studying biographies on Muhammad Ali, Michael Jordan, Roger Federer, Greg Norman, to name a few, I found that they all shared the following common values:

INTEGRITY

RESPONSIBILITY

FAMILY

They also all have individual values that reflect on their own personalities. For example, Greg Norman loved fun and adventure; Muhammad Ali valued his Islamic faith; Michael Jordan loved challenge and self-development. And when it came to being an athlete, they all valued "being the best."

One of the books I read on Muhammad Ali was *The Soul of the Butterfly,* which he co-wrote with his daughter Hana Ali. He wished to be remembered, amongst other things *"as a man who stood up for his beliefs no matter what. As a man who tried to unite all human-kind though faith and love."* He believed in helping other people and treating all people equal, including those who looked up to him.

From his writing, I determined that he valued "humor," "achievement," "respect for humanity," "faith," "love," and "leadership." History proves that Ali fulfilled his value system. His highest values shone through in everything he said and did, and in how he is remembered. During my research on champions, I started to consider the influence of their values on their behaviors. I began to consider the ongoing problems of today's high profile athletes we see all too often in the media.

In Australia, players from all three of the popular football codes—Australian Rules, Rugby Union, and Rugby League—have been highlighted in the media for their problematic off-field exploits. There have been similar problems in the USA with a number of sporting codes and in the UK with football. These exploits occur often at bars, at crazy hours of the night, or with members of the opposite sex.

Michael Jordan, in his book, *Drive Within,* suggested that many of the problems with today's young athletes stem from their being selected early, while still in their teens, based on their "potential." The athletes are offered ridiculous amounts of money to sign with a team or a sport agency, without having to even prove their worth. Compare that to the aforementioned champions, and the work that they had to do to secure both their success in their sport and financially.

I want to point out that tremendous wealth and success often come to these young athletes during a developmental stage when their own values systems are not yet fully formed, and perhaps while they are being influenced by less-than-stellar role models. Being a champion goes beyond physical training. Being a champion is a state of mind that includes what you value, consciously and unconsciously. Developing a set of healthy, strong values that serve the ultimate goals of an athlete can make the difference between being successful and being an "also-ran" in life as in sport.

How often have you heard, or used, the excuse, "That's just how I am!" In actuality, we don't have to resign ourselves to being the way we currently are. Our unconscious mind is a wondrous and flexible thing that can adopt new values at any point. Our priorities are constantly shifting throughout our life anyway—what was important to us at twenty is not as important at forty or fifty.

If your current values are not serving you and the results you want, then you can take steps to make changes. Create a new you. That's what this book is all about. Take on new, positive values and perhaps shift others that sabotage your success or drop them altogether. It's your chance to rewrite your own rules of the game. How do you want to play out the rest of your life? Your career? Who you are within your relationships? The first step to change involves awareness.

If you're not sure of what values your actions and choices have guided you up to this point, it's time to figure that out. Often when you become aware of a problem or a change that needs to be made, you are already halfway to a solution. For example, if you became aware that you were ten kilograms overweight and this was causing health problems, then you would most likely do something about it, such as making changes to your diet. You would be unlikely to make the change if you remained unaware of the problem.

Once you become aware of the kind of thoughts, beliefs, and values that have limited your chances at success, you can go about shifting them, taking on new values to do serve you and your goals—rewriting the rule book that's determined your game thus far. In this next exercise, you will have the opportunity to update your values system, so it's more suited to how *you* want to be and supports want *you* want to achieve.

SUCCESS TRAINING EXERCISE:
Rewrite the Rules

· ·

1. Identify and Rank your Values

The first step to revamping your values system is to identify your current values, not the ones you want going forward, but the ones you hold highest on your list now. What priorities have been dictating your choices and results until now? What values have shaped you?

Take a moment to write down what is important to you in the context of your life. You can do this same process later as applied to your values within sport; then another in the context of relationship, etc. Let's start here with your Life Values. You may have a small list or your list might go beyond the ten spaces provided. That's okay. Just write on the first line below whatever comes to mind when you ask yourself the question:

What's important to me in life?

_____

_____

_____

_____

_____

_____

_____

_____

_____

_____

When you finish listing them, I want you to rank them starting with #1, by asking yourself: *What's most important to me? What's less important?* And so on down to #10, and beyond, if you wrote down more than ten. Write its rank in the column directly next to your list of values. Again, you don't have to think *too* long and hard about it. Just list them in order of what you feel.

2. Re-rank your Values

Now, take a second look and rank those same values again in the third column, this time in order of how they appear in your life— not what you *think* is important but which you actually experience the most in life and the least. For example, you might like to think that wealth is high-ranking; however the absence of it in your life would suggest that perhaps you don't place as much importance on it as other things. So you may have written it down in the first column as your #1 priority, but now as you think about how much time and effort you actually spend trying to create wealth, you re- alize, "not very much!" Then this ranking will be lower.

So, again list them out from 1-10 in order of how much that value is actually demonstrated in your life *right now.* The truth may be different than how you would like it to be.

Like all the work you do here, it is really important to be hon- est with yourself when ranking these values. As with a fitness test that shows you where your strengths are helping you to reach your goals and what you need to work on to improve your performance, this "true values test" will give you a much clearer picture of why you are *not* getting the results you want and what needs to move higher on your list to move you closer to your dreams. The closer the two numbers are to each other, the more likely it is you are rela- tively content with this area of your life. The further apart they are, the more likely this is the value you'll want to change.

Now have a good look at your list and the rankings in the second column and see how it reflects your results. Remember, your top 3-5 values are the ones you manifest the most.

- *Are you happy with those values as you see them on your lists?*
- *Or would you like to see other values appearing in your Top 5?*

For example, when I first did this process for business, I had financial reward ranked very low. I was more focused on working hard, being responsible, making a difference in others' lives, and fulfillment. It was no wonder I wasn't getting far financially and was in a work environment where people were more devoted to helping than getting paid well for it.

I also had a limiting belief that I couldn't have both. I changed that in one powerful weekend at Chris Howard's "Breakthrough to Success," where I confronted my limiting beliefs and values. There were deep hypnotic processes to get to the root of the problem, and these changed me and changed my life, crushing those limiting beliefs that had been holding me back. I emerged with a new set of values where "Making a difference" and "Financial Reward" could sit alongside each other very comfortably. In fact, I discovered that not only are they compatible, they are truly connected, as what better way to make a difference, than to be financially abundant to be able to give my time and money to others.

3. Eliminate Negative Motivation

You want your values to be 100% positive to make them more powerful in propelling you toward your success. Remember how I said that the importance I put on staying "independent" came more from a fear of dependence—that would be a kind of "negative charge" or negative motivation that weakened the force toward my desire to win. It detracted, rather than added energy to move me forward.

Here's another example: if you put wealth in your top 5, is it because you are moving towards a particular lifestyle and what money can allow you to do? Or when you think of wealth do you feel as if, "I have to have money because I don't want to be broke! I hate to struggle financially." That would be a negative motivation because you're more motivated "away-from" poverty than "toward" wealth. Make sense?

Having a negative motivation can keep you from consistently achieving that value. It comes back to the pictures and feelings you are sending to your unconscious—are they of what you *do* want, or are you thinking about all you don't want?

So now you're going to have another look at your values and see what sort of "charge" each value has. Do this with each value as you go down the list. Ask yourself:

- *Does that value inspire me?*
- *Do I feel like I'm moving towards its positive attributes or away from its opposite?*

Consider each of your values now.

1. If the motivation feels positive, put a + sign next to it on that first line.
2. If the motivation feels negative to you, put a – sign next to it.
3. If the motivation feels neutral, or half and half, put a 0 next to it.

Now here's the next-to-last step in rewriting your own rules from now on...

4. Uncover the Belief Behind the Held Value

As you look at your list, you are looking at the unwritten rules of the games you've been playing by, possibly all your life without realizing it! From this assessment you can gain great insight into why you are getting the results you are currently getting in life. Time to rethink it—uncover the hidden beliefs system behind each value so that you can *choose* differently.

Look at each of the values you have placed a (-) negative sign next to, and ask yourself:

- *What must I believe about this value in order to feel this way?*

For example, if your value relating to money is negative, what must you believe about money in order to feel this way? When I thought about my independence, I recognized the hidden belief, "I *have* to do it all on my own." That was limiting how far I could get.

Look for any further information you can get when you compare your values to each other and see if you have a belief that they conflict with each other. If any of those values feel like they cannot coexist in your life, this can indicate another limiting belief, like "I can't have it all." Or for example, individuals might value "family" and "career" but believe that they can't be a mother and be successful in a career at the same time. This is an internal conflict that plays off against each other and sabotages attempts to fulfill either.

Are you becoming aware of patterns of thought and beliefs underlying your values that are playing out in your life? Being aware of your current values and how they affect your results will help you determine what changes you need to make.

You could then study the values of those people you admire: athletes, leaders, business people or anyone who has achieved what it is that you want to achieve. Think about a current role model, someone who has successfully transitioned from success in sport to success in a career beyond sport, or perhaps a popular success like Richard Branson or Oprah Winfrey, or perhaps even a colleague or friend.

Can you imagine what their values must be to get the results they are getting?

5. Choose your New Top 5 Values!

Now choose what you want your new Top 5 to be. After going to personal development courses in 2006, my values completely changed. From a focus on volleyball and fitness, I chose to value making a difference to the world; financial freedom, adventure, relationships, and health. I later adjusted these again to include love, which then further enhanced my life.

Consider reading autobiographies of successful people you admire, particularly those who have achieved what you want to achieve. Here are some suggested values for success, based on my studies of many successful athletes and entrepreneurs:

INTEGRITY	RESPONSIBILITY	FAMILY
RESPECT	FUN	ADVENTURE
GOOD HEALTH	LOYALTY	INSPIRATION
WINNING	FRIENDSHIP	PHILANTHROPHY
CONTRIBUTION	REWARD	WEALTH
CHALLENGE	COMMITMENT	LEARNING/GROWTH

You may have others. It's important to use words that mean something to you. To help you choose your top five values, think about:

- *Which would make you the person you are proud of?*
- *What would get the results you want?*
- *What kind of legacy would you like to leave behind as a result of your life's work?*
- *What would you like to be said about you?*

It may be enough for you to choose your new values and live by them from this moment forward. Consider each chosen value and embrace what that means to you. Allow it to fully ignite your passion for achieving it so that everything you do fulfills your Top 5, like the example from Mohammed Ali's life.

For most people there may be further work needed. Values arise from earlier years and may be ingrained alongside our beliefs. Working with a coach will help you identify limiting beliefs that could hold you back from living life by a better set of values. Remember, your unconscious mind is like the members of the team and determines your performance and results. Unless you make change at that deeper level, you are faced with a constant struggle between captain and team, your conscious and unconscious mind. We all know that makes everything more difficult and less fun.

Summary

✓ Values are what is important to you and determine your behavior and your results
✓ Champions value excelling in life, not only sport
✓ Integrity, responsibility and family values rank high in true champions

It's how you play the game.

• • CHAPTER FIVE • •

LEAP OVER HURDLES

"Life is not simply holding a good hand, life is playing a poor hand well."
• Danish saying

Shattered Dreams

I was ten years old in 1976 when I first dreamt of going to the Olympics. Along the journey to the Olympic stadium in 2000, I acquired many attitudes and skills that I credit with getting me there. It is these same attitudes that have contributed to my success in my new career beyond sport. This next phase in my volleyball career illustrates the kinds of inner resources it took to get there.

Formal beach volleyball competitions and tours started in Australia in 1986-87. I was living in Perth in 1988 when the first Western Australia state competitions were introduced. I had become one of the leading indoor volleyball players in the state and I found the progression into beach volleyball a natural step. My fitness, agility, and leaping abilities were advantages in the sand, and I fell in love with the sport that was so suitable to my skills.

For the first year-round, I played both indoor and beach volleyball as they were played in opposite seasons of the year. I achieved my goals of becoming a regular Australian Indoor representative, played a season in the league in The Netherlands, and then was captain for a brief period in 1993. Towards the end of 1993, it was time to choose between indoor and beach and my decision was clear. When beach volleyball was announced as a medal sport for the Olympic Games in Atlanta, I finally had a real chance of becoming an Olympian. I had enjoyed success the previous summer on the Australian Beach Volleyball tour with a team ranking of number two. I decided to step down from the Indoor program and focus entirely on a beach career.

I qualified with Kerri Pottharst to go to our first World Tour event in Miami, Florida, in February 1994. One of our first games was against the number one Brazilian team, Isabel Salgado and Rosali Timms. Kerri and I went into the game excited and relaxed. This team was one of the best in the world, and no one expected us to do well against them, least of all us. Our game plan was to focus on our own game and play as well as we could.

We started off very well, serving aggressively and putting the ball away easily to prevent the Brazilian's from scoring. It was the old format where a team has to serve to win a point. The first to 15 points wins. We played so well we found ourselves up 8-0, or something ridiculous like that. We kept waiting for the Brazilian's to come back and start playing better. Instead, we kept our momentum and went on to win the match. It was an incredible upset.

Unfortunately, we lost two games in our pool and missed out by a fraction of a point that would have gotten us into the Top 4 in our first international competition. After such an amazing start, we were relegated to the minor play-offs and finished seventh.

Kerri and I continued to play on the World Tour that year, and by the end of 1994, we were ranked eighth in the world. We continued our winning plays in Australia, taking out the first two National tour event titles on the Gold Coast and in Perth. The celebration was short-lived for me though as the very next day, Kerri informed me that she had decided to end our partnership. Kerri chose to continue her campaign to the Olympic Games with Natalie Cook.

The end of this playing partnership in December 1994 was to become a recurring theme for me in my beach volleyball career. This served as a challenge for me to dig deeper within myself and utilize my own inner resources to continue.

The disappointment made me question, *how much do I really want to go to the Olympics?* It was late in the game, mid-season of 1994-95 in my career when I was left without a partner. As I saw my ranking on the World Tour stripped from me, I did the only thing I could...I asked myself the question I'd been asking for the previous eight years, *What do I do now to get to the Olympics?*

I had three viable options of players with whom I could play at the time, and I decided that the best thing for me was to move to Sydney to play with Jacqui Vukosa. Jacqui had played internationally but had incurred several injuries recently that prevented her from playing. She also had a great deal of experience and a personality going for her. This led me to believe that we could do very well together on an international level. Jacqui and I were of a similar stature, or should I say "vertically challenged." We chose to look at this though as an asset rather than a handicap. We used it, in fact, as our strength in terms of our agility and our fitness. From our point of view, we believed it would serve us very well together.

The Asian tour at that time was well organized and provided an opportunity for Jacqui and me to excel quickly and win some prize money. We chose to commit to this tour, so we were also able to then secure a financial sponsor, Cathay Pacific. This made playing international beach volleyball even more financially viable for us. It was a successful venture for us. We went on to win most, if not all, of those tournaments in that year and were crowned Asian Champions in 1995. Jacqui and I also spent three weeks in Hong Kong training and doing promotions for the tournament there. The World Tour was not very extensive at that time, with only six events that year. Our success on the Asian tour, however, did not translate to success on the challenging World Tour and our results put us far outside the reach of our top two Australian teams. With only two teams from each country qualifying for the Atlanta Olympics, our chances of making it were slim.

Reassessment

With the summer season finished and our 1996 Olympic hopes dashed, it was time to once again reassess my situation. I still had the burning dream to qualify for the Olympics and the strong belief that I could do it. I now turned my sights on the 2000 Sydney Games. The first question was *how,* and more specifically *with whom* could I continue my journey?

There was a very talented indoor volleyball player who had just started playing on the beach—Angela Clark. Angela lived in my home city of Brisbane, plus had the advantage of being tall, which meant that she could act as a blocker while I focused on the defensive play in the backcourt. I moved, once again, this time to Brisbane to continue following my dream. It was an easy move to return to my home state, and I even chose to move back in with my parents on the Gold Coast, just an hour's drive south of Brisbane.

We were supported by the Queensland Academy of Sport, which meant we now had a coach. This proved a great help since Angela was new to beach volleyball. The new partnership was reasonably successful. We had a lot of potential, and we were making some progress with a 5th and a 7th on the World Tour amongst our results.

We were also supported by Team Australia Beach Volleyball and included in frequent training camps at the base in Adelaide. It was during one of those camps that my life dramatically changed.

A Major Upset

The year of 1997 was a year that rocked my stability and had me questioning my dreams and aspirations for the very first time. While preparing for a World Tour event to be held in Melbourne, I received a phone call from my father. Mum and Dad were unable to come to Melbourne as planned to watch me compete in the World Beach Volleyball Tour event...Mum was sick.

There were more questions than answers. It started with fatigue and back pain, then grew to severe headaches and throwing up. When all the food had come up, the dry retching continued. An ambulance trip to the hospital's emergency department revealed nothing, and Mum was sent home to rest. Meanwhile, the headaches continued to get worse and were accompanied by dizziness with any sudden head movements.

As I got off the phone, the sinking feeling in my stomach told me that this was really serious. Dad told me not to worry though, and I stayed in Melbourne to compete. I was distraught, but the competitor in me, as well as my practical nature, took over—I managed to focus on the tournament.

By the time I arrived home, Mum had been sick for six days with no improvement. This was the start of further tests followed by hospitalisation and deterioration of her condition. One week, one bone scan, a lumbar puncture, an angiogram, and a thyroid scan later, Mum was recovering with fewer headaches and increased strength and coherency. The diagnosis appeared to be threefold—minor bleeding in the brain; an overactive thyroid, *and* some small bone tumors in the spine. Three different problems at once was a rare coincidence. Two maybe, but three!! The tumors in the thoracic spine were considered secondary to the breast cancer that Mum had had thirteen years prior. Though the doctors tried to make a connection between each of the illnesses, the activity in the brain appeared to be unrelated to the cancer.

Mum was able to come home after seventeen days of hospitalization. Twenty-three days after first falling ill, her spirits were up, and we had high and positive expectations, particularly with alternative therapeutic methods. Dad was a naturopath, passionate about the cures for cancer that existed outside mainstream medicine. This was our family's approach to health. We still had to prepare ourselves for a long road ahead with rest and therapy. My life very quickly took a turn. Accustomed to training every day, my days now revolved around Mum, with all my focus now on her and my family. I squeezed in time for a few gym sessions, but that was all. For once, training took a backseat, and it was not a concern.

Mum had been home six days when my distraught father wakened me at three in the morning. She had had a sudden relapse and was taken by ambulance back to hospital. When the results came through, they were not good. This time it was discovered that the lesion in the brain was cancerous, and it had grown rapidly in the previous two weeks. It was behind the cerebellum or brainstem area, which is in the centre of the brain and very difficult to access due to the positioning and the sensitivity of the brain tissue.

Our family did a lot of talking in those days. We didn't keep the diagnosis from her as we knew she had to come to terms with it. The first few days Mum was very brave, keeping her emotions in check, not allowing us to see how it fazed her. Gradually we were able to coax out the tears and let her know it was okay to feel the grief.

Reading *Chicken Soup for the Surviving Soul* with tales from survivors of cancer marked the beginning of my search for spiritual understanding in my life. Sharing the stories of survival with Mum helped her come to grips with her own condition. From this, she was able to open up a little more about how she felt and perhaps reach some peace. It was a healing time for us all as we all searched within ourselves and deepened our relationships to each other.

After some initial progress, her condition then continued to deteriorate. She lost coherency in bouts, and it became increasingly difficult to hold conversations with her. Nevertheless, the doctors permitted us to discharge Mum from the hospital and continue the treatment at home. It was a tireless attempt to help Mum's recovery, and ultimately it seemed that it did not matter. A strong spiritual healer, Bobby Running Fox, attended to Mum and felt the pain of her childhood. He helped the mind and body to become one so that the spirit could go on peacefully, whether that was to return to us or to leave. I believe that Mum's spirit had already chosen to end this life. The conscious mind may have wished otherwise, however, the struggle was too much.

Throughout these weeks of illness, I stopped my rigorous volleyball training, taking time-out only to maintain my fitness as best I could. It was difficult though to train without my partner or coach. The rest of the Australian volleyball players were in Adelaide, at the National training facility. There came a time when I questioned how long I could put off returning to training. What if Mum's sickness continued on for months? I had international competitions coming up in May and June and needed to be ready. Years of training and commitment had hardened my focus on the practicalities and what needed to be done.

With the blessing of my Dad and family, I chose to return to Adelaide. Dad still had plenty of support from my family, friends, and Bobby Running Fox, who had made a big difference in our situation, providing invaluable support and comfort. He introduced me to *Conversations with God,* a book that finally gave me some direction in my beliefs on spirituality and the essence of being alive here on earth. It also helped me to realize that Mum's time here was perhaps over and that we needed to "let go" in order for her to continue her journey, in another plane. Dad came to understand this too.

I had not been in Adelaide even a week when my playing partner, Angela Clarke, woke me up in the early hours of the morning. I had left my mobile phone in her room, and it was ringing. I guess someone was making sure I would not be alone when I received this call. It was Dad with the news I didn't want to hear...Mum was gone.

I coped well in the beginning, reasoning that death was in fact the best thing for Mum, that she was no longer in pain, and we need not be sad for her. This was a feeling that would continue in the weeks ahead. Yes, I missed her greatly. She had been my best friend, but I knew she was in a good place now.

Here is an excerpt from my diary:

"It is now nearly two months since Mum left us and sadly life continues on at the same pace. Most days appear normal, especially since I am overseas and not confronted with the truth of her absence. But lately I've been down and I feel the loss of her confidence - being able to share my thoughts and feelings with her. She would always know what to say, being sympathetic and not trying to offer solutions when there are none. The hardest part is sticking to the belief that she is with me. In my heart I know it is true but when things are not working out you can't help but ask, "Where are you? Why aren't you protecting me?"

But, you have to take responsibility for your own emotions. Only yourself can choose to feel the pain or the happiness. I must remind myself of this if I am to go forward. But not today."

Despite my stoic response initially following Mum's death, my emotions caught up with me in the years afterwards. I missed the opportunity to share my joys and my despairs with my closest confidant. When Mum died I lost a great part of me. How I experienced my sporting triumphs and losses would never be the same again.

Getting Back In The Game

The experience changed me in some essential ways beneath the surface that ultimately affected my game. I continued on my journey of volleyball with a different outlook on life. Reading *Conversations with God* had changed my perception of the world around me. I started to become aware of how my thoughts and emotions influenced my results. It was a real awakening to discover how much I could affect change by the way I viewed things, yet I had difficulty putting the concept into action and there was little to show in my results. Instead, I continued to struggle for awhile.

I felt good about the prospects for Angela and myself, but at the end of 1997, there were once again changes in teams and partnerships. By this time in Australian volleyball, it wasn't just the players who were making the decisions; the coaches were having the major say in who played with whom. At that point in my career, the message that I was hearing from my coaches was that I didn't really have a strong future in international beach volleyball. New partnerships were formed, and I was left out in the cold, the odd-woman out.

Falling down, yet again, I had to get back up and find a new partner. There were still a few partners available to choose from so I still had hope. Nicole Sanderson had recently returned from fulfilling an Indoor Volleyball university scholarship in the United States and offered the possibility of a long-term option. Nicole and I joined up for the 1997-98 national tour with plans to play on the world tour. We did reasonably well considering Nicole was new to the beach game but still struggled to consistently make top four. Throughout the summer I was conscious of the coaches speaking regularly with Nicole about her playing options. They could see the potential in her game and no doubt were considering what her best options were. It disappointed me that I never seemed to get that conversation with the coaches, about what was best for me.

My suspicions were confirmed mid-season when Nicole decided to split with me for another partnership. To me, it seemed that I was being edged out by the coaches, who just didn't believe I was good enough. I remember receiving a letter from one of the coaches shortly after the split that was highly critical of aspects of my game. It was traditional feedback informing me of the part of my game that was bringing my performance down and preventing me from gaining ground in my athletic career. Though the advice was likely intended to be helpful, I perceived the undertones to be accusatory and more destructive than constructive.

The letter did ignite my competitive edge for the next tournament as I was determined to go out and prove them wrong, to show them that I was good enough. The following week in Perth was a nice boost of self-esteem for me as a Swiss partner and I made a convincing tournament win for my third Australian title. We played in the final against the New Zealand team, and for that moment I felt a bit of vindication for myself. Unfortunately, I was not able to repeat that success in the next tournament, and we bombed out in the semi-final. With the end of the Australian season and no Australian beach volleyball partner, I started to reconsider my future. I began to wonder if I was pursuing a dream that was somehow misguided. *Were the coaches right?* For the first time in my life, I began to question if I had been fooling myself all along about my Olympic dream. I seriously began to consider other options for my future. Physiotherapy? Sports marketing? What else could I do?

Meanwhile, I was continuing my pursuit of personal development and spirituality. As a result, my thought processes and beliefs about what I considered possible were changing. I even visited a clairvoyant at that time who painted a picture of my future without volleyball—it was not very inspirational. He envisioned me settling down, getting a regular job in an office, and living in a granny flat. Ironically, by portraying such a lifeless future for me, his words actually helped me tremendously.

I simply couldn't accept the vision of myself settling down and settling for less. I couldn't bear the idea of watching the Olympics in 2000, wondering *what might have happened if only...* It stirred so much inside me, I responded by dedicating myself 100% to my dream. I had to keep playing volleyball. I had to take the next opportunity to see what I could do. I didn't want to be left with that question. I took charge of my fears and doubts and got back in the game.

. . . .

WINNING POINT #5:
Play Like a Winner

"A winner for me is someone who walks off the court and you can't tell if he won or lost. He carries himself with pride either way."

• Jim Courier

Do you remember in your sport how well you competed when you were in a good mood compared to when you were in a bad mood? How about the difference in your results when you felt anxious versus unbeatable? You can probably remember times when you felt like you were in "the zone." The "zone" has been described as being in a state of "flow," a state from which everything becomes easy, where you can have the powerful sense that, "I can't miss!" or "I can't lose!" In his book *Flow,* Mihaly Csikszentmihalyi described these optimal states of performance as being in a state where the experience is an end in itself. During flow, an individual loses self-consciousness. Enjoyment becomes about being in the moment, not dependent on extrinsic rewards such as trophies and prize money. It used to be thought that the optimal playing zone was magical and elusive and came only by chance. Now, it is believed that, through mind mastery, this mental state of flow can be achieved with intent and with consistency.

I was coaching a golfer once who was having difficulty performing consistently on the green, so I asked him to rank his confidence levels from one to ten and give me the reason why he felt what he did. Every time he stepped up for a hole, I asked him, "What's your confidence level right now?" His answers always varied between a six and eight, and he would say, "I'm confident on this hole because I like this hole," or, "I'm confident because I've been hitting the ball pretty well now." Or, if the confidence dropped off, "I missed that past drive, so I'm less confident. Now I'm down to a four."

He was allowing each result to influence his self-perception and expectations. Of course his game was inconsistent! His results were all over the map because his emotions were all over the map.

If we always let our recent experience dictate our emotions, we're allowing the past to determine our future.

Overcoming Upsets

Can you imagine if there was a way you could consistently use the power of your emotions to play like a winner? What if, instead of allowing your internal states to create more upsets in your game, in your business and in your relationships, you were able to access your internal states like an energy-source to give you force, power and direction? You *can* actually use your emotional states as a tool to impact your behavior and direct your results.

Think of emotions as a valuable resource—they can help determine how well, or how poorly, you perform at anything.

But how can you determine your emotions? Don't they just come and go depending on circumstance? No, emotional responses are entirely dependent on the "meaning" you've ascribed to the circumstance to which you're reacting. It's what you decide about any given situation that will then create the resulting emotion. You can become a master of your emotional state when you learn how to choose your responses.

Consider you're driving to work one day...you're sitting in peak-hour traffic, but you're feeling great, you turn on the radio, and nothing can change how you're feeling. You just listen to the music, and the traffic doesn't matter. Your day runs smoothly; you can handle anything that comes your way. The next day, same traffic, and you get up on the wrong side of the bed...suddenly you're going in and out of traffic, changing lanes. Your different response changed your actions. You started driving more aggressively. Once you got to work, everything and everyone bothered you. On some bad traffic days, your whole perception of the world can change for the worse! And this can change the results you get that day—colleagues may respond to you differently, deals may prove more challenging and you may not be motivated enough to finish work projects on time. Even traffic is not necessarily a "bad" thing, unless you've decided it means, "life is a struggle," or "I'll never be successful at this rate!"

Many people allow their emotions to control them. Successful people are able to control their emotions.

Meanings Make The Difference

Here's the same cause and effect chain of events from Chapter One, to remind you how "meaning" and "emotions" affect the formula for success:

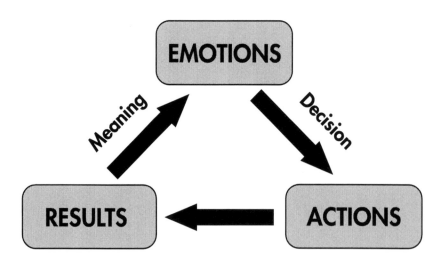

This winning formula works in sport and away from the sporting arena, in business, in life, everywhere you may find yourself—the idea is, rather than react to a situation or emotional trigger, you decide what emotional state you need to be in to reach your goal. Whether it's feeling confident, powerful, or happy, it's up to you to get yourself there so that you're 100% resourceful to make the winning plays in life.

I once had a coach who recommended, "When you're going back to serve the volleyball, imagine you just served a series of aces." Do you think I was in a more positive state when I did that? Yes! Because it kept me feeling confident. If I wound up for the next serve while still thinking about my last serve being an error, would I be more likely to serve another error? Yes.

Imagine Yourself Succeeding

You're mind doesn't really know the difference between real or imagined. That means, each and every moment of the day is another chance to imagine you winning. Put yourself in the best emotional stance possible. Whether it's making a winning pitch at a meeting, setting up a profitable business, or starting a new career after sport, you can improve your chances of achieving your goals by improving your state. There is great benefit in the saying, "fake it until you make it." It just means, you may not be there yet, but if you can get there in your mind first, you've put yourself ahead of the game in terms of seeing your goals through to fruition.

When I first started speaking in front of small groups of people, I didn't know if I was any good at it, if I would fail miserably, or if anyone would even be interested. One thing was for certain: I didn't feel confident right off the bat. But, even with my inexperience, I figured that if I *acted* confident I would at least be more likely to come across confident, which might improve my chances of success. It worked! Most people thought I'd already done a lot of public speaking. I must have convinced myself pretty well. I have used this in many situations from interacting one-on-one, business meetings, to speaking in front of thousands of people.

If you mastered your emotional state during your sporting career, then you already possess a valuable skill you can take into life after sport. When you are in control of your emotions, you are in control of your results. Empowered emotional states are useful for:

- Interviews
- Meetings
- Networking
- Cold Calling
- Sales
- Parents interacting with kids
- Dating
- Team building

This list is far from exhaustive but I wanted to give you some idea of times when it would be more useful to be proactive in your response rather than reactive. Can you think of any particular situations right now in which it would be useful for you to be the master of your emotional states? In what area of your life and career would mastering your emotions help you get better results?

If managing your emotional reactions is not your strong suit, you can develop the skill now through training your mind to be more resourceful. How do you do it?

Master your Emotions

First, decide on the ideal state that would best serve your success in that area.

Too many people out there trying to succeed are letting their emotions get the better of them by thinking that some external situation or person can decide their emotional responses for them. Think about it—have you ever said, "Oh, he makes me mad," or, "That makes me mad," or, That upsets me"? Just as you couldn't do anything to change what they did or what occurred, no one and nothing can *make* you feel or do anything—you *always* have a choice when it comes to how you want to respond to them.

What emotional state would improve your performance? Choose the states that would enable you to be at your best. If you're not sure, think of an area in which you allow your emotions to run you, whether it's panic, stress, doubt, worry, etc. Then imagine the opposite of that.

The optimal emotional state will vary from person to person. In tennis, Chris Evert-Lloyd was renowned for being very cool and collected, not showing much emotion. She was the ice queen. Compare that to the revved-up emotion of Lleyton Hewitt, or Marcos Baghdatis, or John McEnroe—they really had to be fired up to play at their most competitive. So the state you choose to propel you toward your greatness will be unique to you.

The following emotions, and more, can help you get the results you want:

CONFIDENCE	STRENGTH	POWER
PLAYFULNESS	PASSIONATE	COMPASSION
RESOURCEFUL	CREATIVE	

Once you know what your desired emotional state is, then what? How do you actually get in to that state? Do you just cross your fingers and hope "it'll be right on the night?" Do you let it just happen by accident, to be in that emotional state?

I will show you a way you can access a range of empowering

emotional states in an instant by creating a physiological "trigger" for the particular set of positive emotions you choose. This is from traditional NLP (neuro-linguistic programming) and is called a "resource anchor."

An anchor is a link between a physiological stimulus and an emotional state. For example, a certain smell may trigger a strong memory of a person. A song may induce happiness or sadness, depending on the memory attached to it. Perhaps you have heard of the research of physiologist Ivan Pavlov, renowned for his work in "classical conditioning." In the late 1890s, he conducted experiments in which he rang a bell or tuning fork every time dogs were being fed. Consequently, this created an association within their physiology between salivation—their natural response to food—and the ringing sound. After some time of "conditioning," the dogs continued to respond to the sound of the bell, and presence of laboratory assistants in white coats, by salivating, even in the absence of food.

We all have responses that are similarly illogical, yet natural in that it is a neurological trigger response anchored to a past event. Emotional eating such as binging is an example of an inappropriate anchored response, in the sense that it doesn't actually help you to get you what you want. Feelings of insecurity can trigger an intense desire to binge eat so you actually put on weight when your goal was to lose weight. Knowing that habits are connected to emotional and physiological anchors enables us to use anchoring consciously as a technique to get the opposite effect—to empower us toward healthier actions, rather than disempowering behaviors.

Healthy Positive Anchors

Most top athletes have at least one routine they like to utilize to prepare them for a game or a competition. This routine helps to anchor in a positive, resourceful state to go for the next point. As an athlete, you may already have a mental routine you use to get yourself into the optimal emotional state to compete in your sport.

In beach volleyball, I used to clap my hands together followed by a light double fist action in preparation for the next serve from my opponent. Think of some gestures you have used or you've known other athletes to use to improve their performance—a fist pump in the air, three bounces of the ball, a spin or two of the racket—these are all examples of positive resource anchors.

Gestures, mental routines and other physical anchors can be used in any area of life. I use one when I want to prepare to make cold calls. I need to be in a highly aware, positive emotional state to effectively speak with a prospective client or business partner. I would rather be prepared, than rely on luck to convey myself confidently and seem knowledgeable.

SUCCESS TRAINING EXERCISE:
Create a Greater State!

Here is a technique to create a resource anchor that will move you quickly into the desired state you want to hit your goals. Once you've established the positive emotional trigger, you can use it for public speaking, job interviews, business meetings, dating, confrontations, negotiations, or team building, essentially anywhere that you want to have a positive result.

1. Choose your ideal empowered state and design the anchor

Once you've chosen the state that works best for you, you can create kinesthetic anchors using the sense of touch to produce that desired emotional state. The anchor is the gesture or part of your body that you contact to access that great state. For example, you might pinch your earlobe between your thumb and index finger, or press your wrist or hold your hands a certain way. Other suggested body parts to press firmly to create a "trigger" include the middle of the sternum, the point of the elbow, the small pinkie knuckle.

The criterion for your anchor is that it must be a unique part of the body that is not frequently touched. Frequent contact with your "anchor" would dilute the power of the anchor over time as it accumulates other associations over time. So, choose an area that is rarely contacted and use it only to put you in resourceful states.

The area must also be easily and consistently accessible. For example, the underside of the forearm may be rarely touched but unless you have a specific freckle or spot, it is unlikely that you are going to contact the same spot each and every time. Since it's a kinesthetic trigger, you must be able to replicate the exact same response each time.

You may also choose to do a particular strong movement that is anchored into your emotional states, for example, a fist pump action or a double click of the fingers. Once you have chosen the anchor you can then proceed to establish it as your resource anchor.

2. Get yourself into state

Start the process by first getting yourself into the desired state, such as confidence—if you've ever experienced this heightened emotion in the past, then you can recreate it simply using your memory and imagination. It's more powerful if you remember a *specific* time that you were especially confident, then imagine, as if you were right there, feeling that heightened level of confidence again. As you feel that confidence rise within you, maintain it long enough to set your resource anchor by touching the body part or doing your chosen gesture/action. This creates the physiological and psychological association between the heightened state and the touch. The body/mind and emotion form the connection that will still be there for you later when you need to access that emotion.

3. Set the anchor

Two keys to make this process work successfully for you:

- The higher the intensity of the emotion, the more successful the anchor will be.
- Make sure you only hold the anchor while the emotion is strong. Let go or stop the anchor before the emotion drops off.

Repeat the process a number of times. The more you do it, the stronger the anchor will be. I suggest you repeat each desired emotion three times to create the strongest powerful resource anchor possible.

Once you have created the anchor, then all you have to do the next time you need to be in that powerful positive state is fire off the anchor by repeating the touch or gesture. The physiological memory of the state you created will flood the mind again to prepare you for a repeat performance of the previous positive experience...you will suddenly find you have full command of that same resourceful emotional state!

Note: This is especially effective to do just before you know something will predictably trigger off a negative or unhealthy response in you. This way, you start to replace old bad habits with new healthy ones. Instead of you and your performance level being at the whim of your emotions, you are now able to use them to your advantage in the game of life!

 To help you create a resource anchor for yourself, I have a recording that will help you get into a powerful resource state. As a free gift for purchasing this book, you can download from my website the recorded process that will talk you through the resource anchor process step-by-step.

Download your copy at **yourgift.successbeyondsport.com** to **Create your Greater State!**

Summary

✓ Be aware of how your reactions to situations and people are affecting your results

✓ Remember, an upset in a game or in a career is only an upset if you let it be in your mind

✓ Master your emotional states to produce better actions by using a resource anchor

It only takes an instant to turn around an outcome.

CHAPTER SIX

DEVELOP A DREAM TEAM

"Coming together is a beginning. Staying together is progress. Working together is success."

• Henry Ford

The Final Straight

I put my hand up again for selection on the Australian team early 1998 and was paired with Sarah Straton as the fourth-ranked Australian team.

Interestingly, I had actually met and played with Sarah several years earlier in 1991 upon first returning from The Netherlands. I had also considered her as a potential partner when I split with Kerri Pottharst later in 1994. By 1998, Sarah had really improved her coordination and control in the sand. She was a very strong player who had even won a Bronze medal at a world tour event in Japan. At 6′2, her stature made her one of the tallest players on the world tour. We had a good relationship, knew each other well, and yet, I felt that putting the two of us together was more the result of our being the last two players left after the other teams were formed, as if we were the two misfits. This was a perception on my part; one that I suspect ultimately determined my reality.

I saw that we had potential, and Sarah had the height. I didn't have a lot of trust in Sarah though. We both had strength and agility, but I didn't feel that we were getting the results we needed to go all the way. By the end of 1999, we were finishing up a fairly ordinary year, and I just wasn't satisfied with our performance. We were unable to finish beyond 17th and my relationship with Sarah had deteriorated, due in large part to my lack of trust in her. We were struggling, and I made the difficult and painful decision to split with her.

The partnerships required in beach volleyball are unique relationships in the world of sport. Beach volleyball is classified as a team sport, but there are only two people with the demands to make the team function well and succeed. There can be no substitutions during the game, and a team must stick together to qualify for major events, including the Olympic Games. Beach volleyball encompasses all the characteristics of a "team," requiring skills of communication, role play, shared goals, and commitment. There is a working relationship, both on and off court, in preparing for training, competing, as well as working with the coach, sponsors and other stakeholders.

There is also the social relationship to consider. Beach volleyball partners spend a lot of time together out of necessity. Traveling on the world tour non-stop for four months means you need to have a good understanding of each other. Ideally, you understand each other's expectations in terms of spending time together off the court. Being partners doesn't necessarily mean being best friends or even friends at all. Many of the men's teams are very good at treating beach volleyball as a business. I can think of a number of teams that have no time for each other off the court, and some even hate each other, but they are able to put their personal differences aside on the court and play very well together. The Laciga brothers from Switzerland did not talk to each other, even when they were playing, and yet they consistently ranked in the world's top five men's beach volleyball teams.

There are not many women's teams that can pull this off. Women want to be friends, and often any personal differences off the court can spill over onto the court and, ultimately, affect the team's performance. Traveling around the world together, sharing rooms and secrets, can turn into a relationship with all the demands of a marriage. Playing partnerships are often based on playing ability, and yet it's the personality traits that often make or break the team.

Although I really wanted to get to the Olympics, this decision to split with Sarah was really difficult for me. I had been the one on the receiving end of so many splits in the past, and now I was instigating it. My reasoning was based on my observations of others who had gone before me, who had all seemed to achieve better results by initiating a split. I thought that maybe there was something in this for me to learn. If this was the formula required to become a champion, then I would have to do whatever it took. If I was going to make it to the Olympics, I couldn't afford *not* to make the tough decisions.

Another part of my reasoning for risking the change of partnership was my belief that enjoying the journey is as important as the destination. The way we were playing and getting along at that point did not warrant the end goal, as far as I was concerned. I preferred the risk of not reaching the destination for the sake of having a better journey. It was a particularly distressing time, and I don't feel particularly proud of the way I handled it.

I made contact with my old partner Angela Clarke, who had just returned from an injury. She was keen to get back on the tour and attempt to qualify for Sydney, so she immediately took me up on my offer to play together. I didn't fully appreciate the extent of Angela's previous injuries though and was surprised when it turned out that, in fact, she was not yet fit to train, let alone play in competition. Our plan to go to Brazil fell apart. Our coaches put pressure on Sarah and me to keep playing together because they felt we had the results to qualify as the first Australian team in the Olympics. We had already played six qualifying tournaments together and needed eight minimum to be in the run for the Sydney Olympics. With other recent team changes, Sarah and I had maintained the longest standing partnership at the time and were closest to achieving eight tournaments together. Sarah and I had little choice but to play another tournament together. We went to Salvador, Brazil, to pursue that goal.

Our preparation wasn't ideal, and the attempted split had created more tension, so we failed to win a game, finishing 25th. It was time to rebuild our team, so Sarah and I played the Australian summer of 1999-2000 together. It was a rewarding season for us. We made a couple of finals on the main Australian tour, including that season's Australian Open.

That summer we also played in the promotional "One Summer" competition. This was a mix of sports combining Surf Lifesaving, Triathlon, Swimming and Beach Volleyball. It was more exhibition than serious competition, with only four teams playing in the beach volleyball, and games shrunk in size to keep the public interest. The format seemed to suit us. Sarah and I made the finals in two of the four competitions, gaining good TV coverage. We then finished the domestic season, winning the final tour title on the Gold Coast, taking advantage of the absence of a couple of the top teams. The winning feeling was a positive one we took to Vitorio, Brazil, at the beginning of the 2000 World Tour with anticipation of better things to come.

Unfortunately, we were unable to maintain our winning ways on the international scene and once again left Brazil without a win. Despite the loss, this time we were in better spirits, having redeveloped trust and friendship during the summer. We were hopeful and committed to working together to qualify for the Olympics. Despite working with different coaches, working on our fitness, and our relationship and communication skills, our results did not appear to improve. Perhaps we were playing better, but then so were other teams. We struggled to get beyond the first day of competition but still remained in contention to qualify for the Olympic Games.

As hosts of the Olympics in 2000, Australia was granted an extra qualifying spot in the final list of 24 teams. That meant, if two teams from Australia qualified by being in the top 23 ranked teams in the World, Australia could have a third team in the Games. The ranking of the third team did not matter.

Two other teams were doing well on the World Tour and were easily within the top ranked teams in the world. Pottharst and Cook were Australia's number one team, having rejoined forces, and had a number of bronze medals in the lead up to Sydney. Pauline Manser and Tania Gooley also had some good results, including second place at a world tour event. Sarah and I were competing mostly against another Australian team than with the rest of the world, for that third spot. Angela Clarke had recovered sufficiently from her knee injury and was playing with another ex-partner of mine, Nicole Sanderson...they were the team putting pressure on us for that third position at the Olympics.

Nicole had also returned from injury after a serious ACL tear put her out of competition for a year. She was only into her third tournament of the 2000 season when disaster struck again in Toronto. History repeated itself with another ACL tear, this time to the other knee. Sanderson and Clarke were out of the race. We were going to the Olympics.

From that day on, our focus changed to hit our new goal—Sarah and I not only wanted to qualify, we wanted to improve our ranking to be higher within the top 24 ranked teams that qualified for Sydney. This was not only for self-pride but would also help our seeding for the competition. But the pressure was off, and we made little progress toward that end. We continued to finish 17th or 25th in competitions regardless of whether we had a bad draw or good draw against teams we could beat. Some people play with more freedom when there is nothing to lose. This didn't seem to happen for us. It was more the case that the urgency to do well was taken away, and it didn't matter whether we performed well or not since we already knew we were going to Sydney.

Diamonds are formed under intense pressure, and the same could be said for results. Pressure can be a good thing to push you towards stepping up and achieving more. Sarah and I had only our internal pride pushing us, and that wasn't enough to push us towards even higher results. Our ranking going into the Olympic Games was 23, so we had achieved our goal of qualifying in our own right.

It was time to fulfill the dream...September 2000 I was going to Sydney to prepare for the Games, not only with Sarah but as part of the Australian Olympic beach volleyball team! It was persistence and a belief in ourselves that enabled Sarah and me to get to the Olympics. We got there together as a team.

• •

WINNING POINT #6:
Be a Team Player

"Synergy is the highest activity of life; it creates new untapped alternatives; it values and exploits the mental, emotional, and psychological differences between people."

• Stephen Covey

The best kind of teamwork feels like an efficient synergy, a dynamic joint effort in which the best performances are brought out of each team member. The best teams know how to work together as one toward a single shared goal. If you come from a team sport, then you are already familiar with the workings of a team. You know that this kind of synergy can only come from trust.

Even individual competitors like runners and golfers are still part of a larger team, a club, college, state, or national team. Team and individual players must be able to work well with a coach and perhaps a team manager, a fitness trainer and any number of assisting staff to help achieve a common goal.

While teams do well based on the strength of their individuals, it's also true even in an individual sport such as swimming that each member is strengthened by the camaraderie and association with a larger team. Once they are in the pool, the track or pitted against each other on the tennis court it's "game on!" They know that their finish relies solely on their own performance. Yet, the athletes who excel are those who work together outside of the competitive arena to train, stay fit, and learn from each other.

This also holds true for the most successful people and companies in the world. It has been said that it takes teamwork to make the dream work. No one has ever achieved anything great without the support of others. A team can take various forms from mentor relationships, business partnerships, joint ventures, and cohesive project teams or departments within a large organization.

The important thing for you to realize is that you don't have to achieve your dream on your own. You do have to know how to be a team player though and create a team synergy that works for everyone.

Know When Not To Compete

"Michael, if you can't pass, you can't play."
• **Coach Dean Smith to Michael Jordan in his freshman year at UNC**

Did you know that by flying in a V formation, geese increase their flying range by 71% more than if each bird were to fly alone?

Athletes by their very nature are competitive. I've met only a handful of athletes who are not competitive, who haven't got a competitive bone in their body, and are just doing sport for the love of it. Most top-level athletes, however, need to be competitive to maintain their performance edge. They also need to learn the art of give and take.

I've always been fiercely independent. Even as recently as 2006, I prided myself on my independence, believing that I had achieved so much on my own. Even getting to the 2000 Olympic Games, I remember thinking specifically, *"I did this, I did this myself."* The issues I had with coaches and the loss of my mother in 1997, one of my biggest supporters, gave me even more drive to do it all myself. There was a certain pride in that back then.

I was independent and I was competitive, even off the volley-ball court. It was a struggle for me to enjoy the success of others, including that of my friends. Rather than being happy for them, I was envious when my friends experienced success and I didn't. I was creating, in my mind, a sense of "scarcity of success," as if there were only so much to go around. The problem with this thinking was that the more I resented their success, the more I was focusing on my own lack of success—as you know by now, all this did was produce disempowering pictures and feelings I continually sent to my unconscious mind. Based on what you now know of how the brain's Reticular Activating System works, lack of success would then be all I could experience. Also, according to the Law of Attraction, that was what I would create more of...lack of success.

"If They Can Do It, I Can Do It"

I now come from a sense of abundance, so I actually enjoy seeing friends, and even strangers, succeed. If they have attained something I haven't, I now think it means that, "If they can do it, I can do it!" As a direct result of changing my thinking, I feel much more empowered to go for it because I choose to believe there is room for everybody. Imagining a limitation on success in your mind will create that limitation in your results.

Being competitive and independent also limited me in other ways. My foolish pride and independence stopped me from asking for help. I thought I could do it on my own, but as I've already mentioned, no one has achieved greatness on their own. I did work in teams and was a valued team player, at times even a leader within organizations I worked for, yet I wasn't enrolling people in *my* dream.

I'm now an entrepreneur developing my business as a coach, a speaker, and an internet marketer. There is no way I could do all that without help. I enjoy finding more and more people to support and assist my business with their skills that I don't have. Through business and social networks, I meet people who know someone who, in turn, know someone, etc. I have become more confident in asking help and asking questions to learn what I don't yet know.

Trust Your Teammates

Working together with others entails trust. A lot of the issues I had playing in a beach volleyball team related to lack of trust. I've come to recognize that trust is an ongoing lesson for me. The lessons came in all different forms, and each time I experienced my own lack of trust, I gained greater clarity about myself, which enabled me to live with greater ease in my relationships—with others, as well as with myself.

Despite my partnership history, I didn't identify trust as the problem until 2007 when I received some important feedback from a company where I worked. In a standard company process, employees in my team that I managed submitted individual opinions concerning our relationships at work and, more specifically, my ability as a manager. My colleagues all confirmed support for my knowledge and organizational skills, yet each of them expressed a common sentiment that they didn't feel I truly trusted them.

This was a great shock to me as I felt that I did trust them and wondered what I could be saying or doing that led to them feeling otherwise. I knew that I was pretty tough in what I expected from colleagues, as I placed these same tough standards on myself. These standards included having certain ideas about the time frames and the methods necessary to complete the job. I would never have overtly said that I didn't trust the people in my office. However, I must have been expressing it in my actions or decisions. When I did look deeper, I discovered that my employees were, in a certain sense, correct.

Although it was true that I trusted those on my team personally and their abilities, it was also true that I didn't really trust them to get the job done *my* way. My way included a particular method I expected, and more importantly, a certain speed of delivery of the work. The more I looked into this issue the more I began to realize how much my lack of trust had actually been a theme throughout my life and had created very big problems for me as I had tried to achieve my dreams! I had never really recognized this as a personal stumbling block before.

There were often times when I would be too insistent about the speed or manner in which I thought things were supposed to be done. Although I had previously seen this as a positive quality in myself, I was beginning to see how this was something that was actually detracting from the ability of others to trust in themselves. It was confusing them and slowing them down. My impatience with others appeared as if I didn't trust them. I finally recognized that the patience I needed and the trust they needed went hand in hand. You see, I was in the habit of wanting things to happen right now. I think most people can relate to that—immediate gratification! When they took longer than "this instant," I forgot that things were still happening "exactly they way they are supposed to." I would get frustrated and then throw my trust out the window.

Real trust is when you trust the person *and* the process, regardless of your past experience or beliefs. It's easy to trust when you agree, and so it's not really trust. Being able to let go and trust wholeheartedly, even when you don't agree, now that's trust!

Pass Off the Baton

Every team sport requires at some point that you pass off the baton or pass the ball or rely on the next team member to run the last part of the relay. In life, as in sport, the best results come from being a real team player—letting someone else make the shot, score or be the one to pass the finish line and get the glory. Participating in games and competitions always requires a high degree of trust, as you rely on others to perform as well. This ability absolutely translates to achievement beyond sport as well. In order to allow yourself to trust your teammates at work, you have to trust that the team works, and beyond that, everything works. Take that new belief on and see how it improves the synergy within your team.

I do believe there is a certain order of things in the universe. We aren't truly aware of this order when we are rushing around trying to get everything done on "our time." It takes trust in the process to remember that things will happen at the right time if we will only let them happen their own way. When you actually begin to trust in the order and synergy of life itself, as it includes business, sport, career path, relationships, it's amazing to see how things really do get done in the best possible way.What I learned after watching my situation more closely each year was that letting go of the need to have things happen *my way* showed me how the universe could actually produce better results. When I learned this, it took a big load off my shoulders. It greatly reduced the level of frustration in my life and supported greater and greater levels of success, allowing me to remember sooner each time to let go of my way and trust.

The Effects of Lack of Trust

Looking back over my volleyball career, I don't think I had the level of trust that would have propelled my volleyball career to an even greater level. I didn't trust my coaches. Their behavior, to me, seemed to represent a lack of support. At times, even when my coaches were expressing their support for me, I either didn't believe them or I felt they were only telling me the things they thought would make me happy. I had a negative attitude, and this became a self-fulfilling prophecy. When I failed to believe them, I also failed to believe in myself.

This same problem manifested itself in relation to my teammates. Although I didn't see it at the time, I was failing to trust my fellow partners in many ways, and I often sought to "help" them as if they needed my assistance, more than was actually the case. Instead of allowing them to learn the lessons they needed to learn, I sought to give advice or rescue them when they didn't really need my help. Unconsciously, I was sending out a message that I didn't think they could do the things they needed to do on their own. It demonstrated that I didn't trust them, which likely contributed to their own self-doubt and lack of confidence, perhaps even to their changing partners.

Lack of trust can appear as a need to be in control. Perhaps you know a "control freak" or two. This need to be in control implies that there is only one way to do things. It can be tiring when everything has to be done according to someone's viewpoint. It closes that person off to learning a better, or simply an alternative, way to getting the same result. It also drains the initiative of others in the team.

In *The Speed of Trust,* Steven M.R. Covey wrote how trust directly affects speed and cost within the business arena. Increasing trust improves speed and efficiency and reduces costs. I can see what lack of trust cost me, not only in dollars but in time and relationships. Trusting that someone else can do the job completely, without wasting time micro-managing, makes for better time management. Demonstrating confidence in someone allows them to feel trusted, which also means that individual is more likely to do a better job. When you trust that other members of your team are doing what is needed of them, you can focus on what you are good at and accomplish more.

Many Ways to Trust

Trusting can mean letting go of the need to be "right" or letting go of the need to be "perfect." It frees up so much energy when you realize that everything can be perfect just the way it is. In a game, it doesn't really matter whether the way you win the point is pretty or ugly. What matters is the end result. When you let go of what you expect it "should" be, a space can open up for what it might actually become. This will often be much better in the long run than you thought.

Sometimes you've got to pass the ball to make the play. In business, you've got to share the effort and let team synergy take over.

We all have our own pictures and ideas of how things *should* work. These expectations are often shaped by our beliefs, our values and our upbringing, who we modeled and our learned perception of what's "right." Still, nobody is ever completely right about how it should work because there is no one right way. The sooner you learn this, the better the team can work together effectively.

Become open to other ways of accomplishing a shared goal. Learn from others. Watch and listen. Be flexible instead of always wanting to tell everyone how *you* see it. Learning how to really listen and be receptive to other points of view cultivates higher solutions. Instead of insisting on your point of view, utilize the power of the group mind through brainstorming. Becoming more open to others will actually propel you forward in your life, your business, and relationship success.

I recommend this exercise next time you are listening to someone. It sounds simple at first, but takes skill and patience. Believe me, this communication practice pays off in big ways:

- For at least a minute or twenty, completely let go of your personal view of reality and put aside what you think is right and "true."
- Listen to another person as if you know absolutely nothing on the subject. Listen to them, instead of your own internal commentary, without constantly comparing what they're saying to your own version of "the way things are."

By letting go of your model of the world, you can actually hear them, as if for the first time. Listening like this, you are free to learn something, to see something you hadn't before. It can help you let go of what you're thinking and of what you think you need to contribute to the conversation. For once, let the other person really feel heard!

Rather than jumping in immediately with your own opinion, when you respond, your contribution to your partner will be more like reiterating their words and repeating what you heard them say. You can also ask them some questions to see if you've really heard them in the way they intended. This is a great exercise to develop the ability to trust, be more open and free on both sides. Your partner will also love you for it, and their confidence will soar. It's near miraculous how much real progress you can make in your communication, in your problem-solving, and in generating fresh ideas and true synergy in your professional and personal partnerships. The strength of the team or partnership will grow in leaps and bounds.

Trust comes into play in so many aspects of career and sport, as well as personal and professional relationships, so we will return to the issue of trust again in later chapters. With regard to teamwork, it is important for you to start thinking about your level of trust in others. Have you been burned in the past by someone, and because of that decided, "I can't trust anyone!"? Is it part of your internal dialogue to tell yourself, "Everyone is out to get me," or "I have to do it all myself!" Unfortunately, if these beliefs were developed in sport, they will likely stay with you into your later career and limit you in terms of getting others to help you. If your career is moving forward slower than you prefer, trust issues may be holding you back. Liberating yourself from this old thinking will expand your potential in more ways than you can now see.

If you are constantly busy taking on too many tasks because

you are unable to trust others to do the job, you are causing your-self undue stress and are probably less effective in getting the job done. With time such a valuable commodity these days, you have to learn to trust and delegate to create that synergistic team work, so you can free yourself up to focus on what you do best.

When I first moved out of the house that I owned and gave it to a property manager to look after, I found it difficult to let go. I was still micromanaging, making sure every expense was run past me first for approval. I'm sure they thought of me as their worst night-mare. The fact was, they were the experts and there came a point when I decided to value my time more and let it go. I gave them my trust, believing that they would do what was in my best interests to keep costs down, get a good tenant, and ensure the home was maintained well. They still run things past me, as is customary, but I will generally go with their suggestions. It has worked out well, and perhaps at times I may have paid more than if I had stuck my nose in and questioned things, but that would have cost me time. I have better things to do with my time.

I also recently handed over my bookkeeping. That has had its teething problems and perhaps in the beginning I handed over too much trust. The other side of the coin to trusting others is to do your due diligence. Take responsibility for ensuring that the person you are delegating tasks to has the appropriate capabilities.

Maintain Responsibility

Having trust does not mean letting go of responsibility. In the very beginning of this book, I discussed taking personal responsibility for everything that happens in your life. The same principle applies here—even when delegating, retain responsibility for the project rather than palming it off on another person. At all times you want to avoid blaming another party for things not getting done. One;

make sure that they can actually do what you are asking of them and two; make sure that they clearly understand what it is you want.

Working with others requires good communication, and you need to take 100% responsibility for communicating the details of a task or project. It is no good to say, "...but I told him to do this and this, etc." If that's the case, then you take responsibility for the communication—obviously they didn't understand your instructions, so you simply need to communicate it differently until they understand it.

Whenever I encounter a misunderstanding, I rather ask questions than point the blame. This is more likely to move the problem towards a solution. It is also a human trait that when you blame someone, his or her defenses arise, and when you accept responsibility the other person is more likely to accept responsibility themselves. Does the following sound familiar?

Person A: "It's your fault that...." **Person B** replies defensively: "No, its not!"

as compared to:

Person A: "Sorry, it's my fault, I could have done...." **Person B** replies: "No, no, I did this and should've done...."

I don't believe communication is a 50-50 deal because when you hand over that 50% responsibility, you risk the other person not listening correctly. When both participants in a conversation take 100% responsibility, communication is at its most effective. We have talked about the value of trust, the skill of delegating, and the benefits of developing good communication and listening habits. Put these together with the practice of taking 100% responsibility and you have all the tools you need to create synergistic team effort.

The Four Types of Mates You Need

It is now time to think about *who* can help you get to where you want to go. What sort of help do you need? Who will be on your team?

As an athlete, you had all kinds of people with various skills supporting you to become the best you could be, to fulfill the dream. It is no different in life beyond sport—you don't have to do it all on your own. You can create your own dream team to help you get a new business off the ground, gain ground in an unfamiliar industry, manage projects within a corporation or enjoy any lifestyle you desire. Here are the mates you should consider pulling together to create the same level of success you enjoyed in sport...or greater:

#1: Coach

A personal or professional coach can teach you new skills, train you to optimize your talents, and keep you accountable. How are you coping now without a coach heading up your team? Have you ever tried to stay in the same shape or do drills on your own at the same level you did with a coach? It's hard! I'd even say impossible. I don't think it works for any athlete. Behind every high-achiever there is always someone on the sidelines guiding and supporting them with their wisdom and experience.

Imagine how things might be if you still had someone in your career, and in your relationships, to give you a game plan and help you prepare to play! What if you had someone you respected by your side every step of the way to point you in the right direction and tell you exactly what you need to do in order to achieve your personal dreams? There are many styles of coaches away from the sports field, including life coaches, business coaches, strategy coaches, relationship coaches, and mindset coaches. As a mindset coach, I focus on developing the best possible mindset to produce winning results so people can consistently achieve their goals in career, relationships and in health.

You can achieve much more in life with a coach than you ever will on your own because a coach will keep you moving forward from one step to the next in the right direction until you get where you want to go. A coach will ensure you learn everything you need to from your mistakes and setbacks so they don't repeat themselves. That one person is always there to keep you focused on solutions and improving your weaknesses.

I am a coach. I also *have* a coach. The style of coach I have varies, depending on my needs at the time. Right now I am focused on strategy and fine-tuning better ways to run my business and get my message out to my audience. It's wonderful having an outside viewpoint on what I can do to keep expanding my earnings. We brainstorm more ideas than I could up with on my own. Then I look to others to help me execute them.

#2: Mentor(s)

Having a mentor is usually a less formal arrangement than having a coach. Many successful people are happy and willing to share their knowledge and experience with another keen to get into the same business or profession. As an Olympian I have mentored many an upcoming athlete by sharing my experiences, from life on the world tour to training practices.

Getting a mentor that has succeeded in an area of business that you wish to emulate gives you a perfect opportunity to model that success. To get a mentor, all you have to do is ask! Many people are flattered to be asked. As long as it fits in with their schedule, they will very likely agree to mentor you to some degree. And if you persist and use your team synergy skills you just learned, you may even have yourself a life-long mentor.

#3: Support Crew/Network

Who supports your dream? As athletes, most of us are lucky enough to have a kind of "extended team" of people who follow our progress and even get caught up in our dreams and ambitions, helping us get there in any way they can. These are not just cheerleaders. In the world of business, this is your network.

Surround yourself with people who are willing to stand behind what you do because they believe in you. Go to events, conferences, and clubs where you can rub shoulders with like-minded professionals, especially those with similar goals or life paths with whom you can go the distance together. This becomes a mutual support team, a formal or informal group of people, whom you admire, respect, and learn from. Why hang around people who want to pull you down? Ideally, your time is spent with people "on the same wave-length" who hold you up to a high standard of achievement. Even better, they have surpassed your level of success and inspire you to shoot beyond what you thought possible.

As you grow and transition, developing a new career, you may start to mix in different circles, drifting away from some of your friends. That is a natural cycle. Now that you have left your sporting career behind, you will need to consider the balance between maintaining contact with that lifestyle and creating a new one, to continue to develop a network that supports you. It's not something you need to do dramatically and cut ties with life-long friends, as I've seen some people do. A career beyond sport can be more of a natural progression that grows out of having a new set of clear goals and aspirations. You may, however, need to make tough decisions if a person is constantly draining your energy or is holding you back, feeling like a ball and chain around your ankle.

When I went to my first personal development seminar, my then boyfriend was okay with my going, but he thought it was a waste of time. He thought all that motivational hand-clapping and hugging stuff was ridiculous. As my passion to learn more and more grew, so did the gap between us. As I was studying the success mindset and was keen to apply the tools in all aspects of my life, including relationships, I stayed with my boyfriend. I tried looking at how we related from different angles, tried to see him differently. Eventually, I grew unhappier as my dreams for my own life grew bigger.

There came a point where I realized that if this was as good as it got for us, then I wanted out. The week I left him I felt like I had let go of a heavy weight, which then rocketed me forward. I was so productive and full of ideas that I achieved more in that one week than I had achieved in the previous three months. Surround yourself as much as possible with others who support your goals and dreams.

4: Specialized Support

In sport, there are always doctors, chiropractors, physical therapy specialists, sponsors, media, even concessions staff on the sidelines making sure you get the proper nourishment and replenishment. Who do you need to help you achieve your dream in life beyond sport? They probably won't just be there waiting for you in the wings when you get started. You have to go out and find the right professionals with the skills you need to launch your new career or reach your life goals. Find those with specialized knowledge that you don't have. Communicate what you need. Then find a way to enroll them in your own vision and ideas for the future.

If you are going into business for yourself, think about what kind of specialized support you will need. Do you need partners? Investors? Do you need to have referral partners in another organization to refer business to each other? Do you need financial support staff, an accountant, a financial planner or advisor? As you put together your dream team, you may find that staff or advisors who specialize in accounting, marketing, administration, internet, and website development are critical to your career's growth.

As I mentioned earlier, while it's important to trust, make sure these people closest to you—who have access to the most important information—are worthy of that level of trust. If you're hiring staff or contractors, it's usually best to have them referred by someone you trust or to nurture the trust over time based on their results.

Just a note here: when you are asking advice from your support network or your specialized support...ask the right people! If you want financial or investment advice, don't necessarily go to someone close like a family member or friend unless that person has a proven track record of success in that area. You might be interested in investing in shares, for example, and the friend you ask may have tried it once and lost. They will be advising you to stay clear of shares based on his or her one bad experience. At least if someone is volunteering you advice, ask that person to qualify it, that is, ask *why* he or she thinks that way. It will likely be based on the individual's experience, rather than extensive knowledge in the field. Find someone instead who is well-versed and successful in your area of interest. Better yet, ask several people with specialized knowledge, then weigh out their various opinions. In the end, after getting educated on the subject, use your own best judgment.

SUCCESS TRAINING EXERCISE:
Create Team Synergy

• •

Here is a great opportunity to brainstorm and write down any and all ideas you have about building your team dream. First, take a psychological inventory of how you are around the issue of trust, independence, responsibility, and communication. Ask yourself the following questions to develop greater insight into how well you work with others. Write down the areas you feel you could benefit from working with a coach. Take your time with each response.

Think about the teams you've been on during your life and take a closer look at what created that synergy, what made you a winning team and what factors influenced your losses. Imagine how you could generate that same magic in whatever new field or endeavor you are beginning next. Get your creative juices flowing and write your answers in a notebook if you need more space:

1. How do you feel about delegating tasks?

_____

_____

_____

_____

_____

_____

_____

_____

2. Have you been let down in the past by a team-member?

_____

_____

_____

_____

_____

_____

_____

_____

_____

_____

_____

3. What did you decide as a result of being let down?

_____

_____

_____

_____

_____

_____

_____

_____

_____

_____

_____

4. In light of what you have read and your responses to the questions, what could you decide now that could help you work better/easier with others?

_____

_____

_____

_____

_____

_____

_____

_____

_____

_____

_____

5. What tasks will you now delegate or outsource? What could be better done by someone else?

_____

_____

_____

_____

_____

_____

_____

_____

_____

_____

_____

6. What is the best use of your time? At work? At home?

_____

_____

_____

_____

_____

_____

_____

_____

_____

_____

7. Do you truly listen to what others are saying? Or do you spend more time defending yourself? Or thinking that you're "right?"

_____

_____

_____

_____

_____

_____

_____

_____

_____

_____

8. If task is left incomplete or there is a miscommunication, can you see where your responsibility is in the situation?

_____

_____

_____

_____

_____

_____

_____

_____

9. What are some areas in your career, at work or in your relationships that you'd like to improve? Can you imagine how they might change if you chose to trust more? Listen and communicate more effectively? Take 100% responsibility?

_____

_____

_____

_____

_____

_____

_____

_____

And now, consider who's on your team now? And how could your results improve if you chose different teammates? Who would you ideally like to surround yourself with for success?

Who do you have on your team now?

_____

_____

_____

_____

_____

_____

Who would you like to have on your team?

_____

_____

_____

_____

_____

_____

Summary
- ✓ Learn how to work effectively with others to achieve your dreams easier and faster
- ✓ Trust improves efficiency and results
- ✓ Effective communication is key to working with your team

It takes teamwork to make the dream work.

• • CHAPTER SEVEN • •

FULFILL THE DREAM

"Knowing is not enough; we must apply. Being willing is not enough; we must do."

• Leonardo da Vinci

Let the Games Begin

I still remember the morning of the competition, Day 1 at the 2000 Sydney Olympic Games. I woke up feeling tired with a slight head-ache. We participated in the opening ceremony the night before, which ran late, and then it was an hour drive from the Olympic stadium back to our accommodation. By one in the morning, we were in bed, and I remember thinking as I woke up early the next morning, "Maybe the coaches were right. Maybe I shouldn't have participated in the opening ceremony." The thought quickly passed though as I focused on all I needed to do to prepare for our game that afternoon. Our match wasn't until three o'clock in the after-noon, and our team knew exactly what to do to get ready and get to the stadium.

Throughout the day, I was completely fired up from the atmo-sphere of the night before. Being a part of the opening ceremony was like nothing else I'd ever experienced or have felt again since—it was positively electric, thousands of athletes from all over the world together in one stadium, athletes, like me, who had been training perhaps their whole lives for this opportunity. The sounds, the sights, the sense of unity and heightened competition at the same time, it lit me up from the inside and made everything I'd gone through to get to that moment all worth it.

Still infused the next morning with that incredible sense that I'd finally arrived at my destination, I was now ready. This was my Olympics, and I was ready to play.

Sarah and I had our a pre-game routine down to the minute, so that when we walked into the arena for our ten minute warm-up, we knew exactly that we needed to do to be prepared and ready for the game. We spent the morning reviewing video footage of the team we would be playing against that afternoon. Knowing their game, we felt confident that we knew how to respond to their different playing styles.

We would be up against the number two team in the world, the number three seeds for the competition, Jenny Johnson and Annett Davis from the United States. Our warm-up in a separate set of courts outside Bondi Stadium went perfectly. Our countdown had begun. Sarah and I had done it so many times before that we knew when to run around the court, when to stretch, when to start hitting the ball—we were in perfect sync knowing exactly what to do in the minutes timed down towards entering the Olympic stadium. Then the moment came...a liaison called to us to come in and get ready to walk into the Bondi Stadium.

As we stood there between the stairs about to enter, our Australian team liaison supporters, ex-Australian swim coach, Laurie Lawrence, and racing car driver, Peter Brock , came up to give Sarah and me a special good luck wish. That really gave us a warm feeling that there were so many people behind us, supporting us into this match. What an amazing feeling, running out into the sand in front of 10,000 people ready to watch us—their home team, Australia—play up against the United States team. We were ready for this match, our fans were ready, we had our little fan club in our specially-made yellow T-shirts that said, "Sarah and Netty Support Crew" cheering us on loudly. Sarah and I once again fell into our preparation routine.

The coin was tossed. We had hit our last warm-up serve, the game was ready to begin, and I was back, ready to serve the first ball. Sarah and I were fired up and ready for the games of our lives, to seriously challenge the number two team in the world.

We traded points for points; they would go two or three points ahead, and then we'd come back. My serving was on fire, and I served several aces throughout the game. In particular I remember serving up an ace to tie up 11-11. The veins were ripping out of my neck as I cheered and celebrated. It was 12-13 when I once again served, and we played a rally: we put the ball back into their court, and they struggled to get it up, kept it alive, but not good enough, and the ball went out. As we tied up 13-13 the crowd just ruptured into applause, banging their feet...the noise was deafening. I remember saying to my partner, "Okay, keep focused, keep focused."

Serving for point 14 was oh so close. I read their play and picked up the ball in defense giving us a play on the ball. Sarah put it over deep into their court, but they were able to retrieve it and then hit it away for a winner to save the point. That was our last chance. The next two points went much too quickly. After being so close, all of a sudden it was over. We were so close to an upset win over this team, and then we lost it in what seemed like an instant: 15-13. It had been so intense with our fans on the edge of their seats and with those last two points the opportunity was lost.

We were not yet out of the competition and would get to play again, but Sarah and I had put everything into that first game. It was difficult to repeat the effort on day three against a team from Germany. The way I remember it, we were never really in that match. I did have a few special moments during the game when I felt I had to take some risks. I served aggressively and went for it, breaking the Olympic record for speed. They have a speedometer at major competitions, which measures the speed of the ball from the serve—I served a ball at 81 kilometers per hour. I kept that record for a few days until Kerri Pottharst broke it a few days later. It was one good serve, but we needed more that day.

We had played full out, put all our years of practice into action on the court. It had been an incredible rush, playing out on centre court surrounded by thousands cheering us on. Right there and then after that last game I felt the disappointment of losing. My journey to this point was over. It was later that I would reflect—I was an Olympian, I had fulfilled the dream! It was much more later that I could truly celebrate the achievement.

· ·

WINNING POINT #7:
Make it Happen

"You cannot change anything in your life with intention alone, which can become a watered down, occasional hope that you'll get to tomorrow. Intention without action is useless."

• Carolyn Myss

I hope you realize by now that you can achieve whatever you set your mind to. In previous chapters, you set specific goals for your life beyond sport, or perhaps for your sport career. You also learned a lot about the mindset you need to achieve greatness in any area. You have a whole new set of inner resources at your fingertips now to create the experiences your want. You know how to change any current beliefs, values, decisions, emotions and other thought processes that are not getting you the results you want. And you have the opportunity to "show up" in life, in sport, and in relationships, in a new way that will work for you. Now I want to tell you that none of this is worth anything unless you take action. Put it into practice.

Whatever your future vision for yourself, there is no substitute for getting out there and getting in the game. Even if the idea of starting a new career or learning new skills or entering the corporate world not knowing the rules of the game, is daunting, you still have to play to win.

Before you take action, you need to decide what you are going to do. This sounds like common sense, but remember, I spent a full six years after the Games not committed to anything and therefore not fulfilled. So, when I say "decide," I mean make a firm decision, not a "maybe" or a "we'll see...." I understand you may not know exactly what you want to commit to right now, but you will never find out until you're out there in the game. Until you decide that you are going to achieve a goal, that goal remains a dream.

The decision must then be followed up with a commitment to yourself to do whatever it takes to achieve that goal. If you haven't committed to sticking it through to the end, you are likely to be side-tracked. Obstacles may appear along the way. However, if you get discouraged at points, your decision and commitment will get you through.

As you know from sport, whenever you set a goal, obstacles arise to challenge you. There are opponents standing between you and that goalpost, long distances and hurdles to jump between you and that finish line...they can't stop your drive, but how do you get over them? What are you going to do with the circumstances and people that seem to stand in the way of your success outside sport?

Your response to setbacks and failures along the way will determine your ability to achieve your outcomes. So here are more keys to the success mindset that will keep you on track as challenges arise so that you can go all the way with your dreams:

Keep Your End Game In Mind

I guarantee you there will be distractions along the way. Whether it's someone suggesting the latest get-rich-quick scheme or your reading about other opportunities that pulls your focus off track, these distractions are just there to test your resolve. Are you willing to stay focused on your target or are you willing to sell out on your dream for a supposedly easier path? Every time an obstacle comes along your way, keep asking yourself:

- *How can I get to my goal?*
- *Where do I want to end up?*

I had the pleasure of going on a trip with author and entrepreneur Keith Cunningham. I was a member of Chris Howard's Billionaire Adventure Club, which combined philanthropy and adventure with education, brainstorming, and networking. It was a fabulous experience and a big factor in my rapid development in my wealth mindset and growing business. I went with the club to Peru, including time spent at Machu Picchu. Keith Cunningham joined us as a special guest to provide mentorship and a full-day workshop.

I learned several basic concepts from Keith that I hear clearly in my mind when I am tempted to stray from my path. One of them is, "Get in line, stay in line!" Imagine yourself in a supermarket, and you have a choice of check-out lines to join in order to pay for your groceries. If you are like most people, you will look for the shortest line to join. Now imagine that the line is held up, and because you feel you are not getting anywhere, you jump to another line. Of course you have to go to the back of this new line. As you move along, you notice your original line is moving faster, so you switch lines again, but you can't go back to your original position. You are forced to go back to the end of the line again. We all know this frustrating experience in traffic as well.

This is a wonderful metaphor for what goes on in your career when you switch from one goal to another, one opportunity to another. It may be exciting to keep trying something new, but your progress towards an end goal is likely to be limited, or slowed, as you keep going back to the end of the line to start over. It's only when you persist in the one line, towards the one goal that you will be successful.

Keep your inner-eye on your target and your day-to-day focus on whatever you have to do that's in front of you to get there. Be like the laser beam, directing all your energy in that one direction. Get in line and stay in line until you get what you want. Stay as focused and committed as you were in sport—it will pay off in the same way.

Power Of Persistence

"Do, or do not. There is no try."

• Yoda

The power of persistence to overcome obstacles is awesome. We've all seen the athlete who is short on skill or stature but more than makes up for it in tenacity. I never would have gotten over the setbacks of injuries and partnership changes without persistence.

The important thing to consider is how much do you want your goal? Are you prepared for things to go pear-shaped? If you want to get from A to B, expect to have to go round or over some hurdles to reach your destination. Prepare accordingly—make up your mind that you will persist no matter what. By committing to your goal in this way you will always outlast and overcome anything else.

To have the heart to persist, you need to have an important enough reason, a "why" to reach your goal. When your goal is meaningful, as discussed in goal setting, then that can inspire you to keep going when the going gets rough.

I was so focused on making it to the Olympics; it was like a magnet pulling me through trouble, giving me the courage to keep going for it. Along the way I often reassessed the goals, questioned them, and determined if they were really what I wanted. I believed I had a chance of going to the Olympics, even if nobody else did, and as long as I had even a slim chance, I was committed to going for it.

Think about what you have achieved in your sporting career and where you have demonstrated persistence. You will have persisted at some point—in training, through the hard times and even persistence through the good times, striving to be even better. Draw from this same tenacious drive as you're creating a new life for yourself. In fact, you can create a resource anchor to access that inner-resolve and commitment whenever your persistence is tested.

No Failure, Only Feedback

Here is another belief that can shift your mindset and set you up to succeed no matter what: *There is no such thing as failure, only feedback.*

One can learn the most from one's failures. In fact, we do this from the very beginning of our lives—as babies, we are constantly learning new skills, to sit-up, to crawl, to walk, etc. If we had given up after our first attempt at walking just because we fell down, then we would all be stuck crawling around as adults! Instead, we developed our muscle strength and coordination until we could balance on two feet. As athletes, we are always looking to find what doesn't work so we can try something different that *does*. As adults, we sometimes think we should already know everything. Be willing to continue learning new things, especially if you're beginning a new phase of your life and career. Put this habit into practice in business and relationships, continually honing your systems and communication until you find what works. The cycle of feedback will continue to give you greater levels of success.

Throughout our lives, we are constantly getting results, some we like—especially when they match our goals—and some we do not like. We learn from each attempt, each mistake. Or we give up. Again, that choice depends on what you think that result *means*. As described in Winning Point #5, the meanings you choose to ascribe to any seeming "failures" makes all the difference in how you move forward or not. If your first attempt at having your own business doesn't get off the ground, you have the option of telling yourself, *"I just don't have what it takes,"* or…*"What does that tell me about what I can do differently?"* This second response gives you the advantage of learning something new.

Take responsibility for how you respond to setbacks. Make it an empowering experience for you and others. Be careful because that one decision will determine your next step. Do you continue as you were without changing anything? Or do you adjust your strategy, develop new skills or make some other changes that inspire you to continue striving for your goal? Or do you perhaps take it as feedback that it's time to shift direction? The important thing is that you use it as feedback and not as a sign of failure.

Learning from everything you can going forward will positively affect your outcome and move you further, faster toward your end goals.

Keep Clear Direction

How do you know if a poor result, or a pattern of repeated poor results, is an indication to make some modifications and still continue on the same course? OR an indication to change course altogether?

Firstly, a poor or undesired result is definitely an indication to make some kind of change. Shifting your goals and direction is a valid response to setbacks, just be clear about which goals you truly desire so you can focus all your efforts in that direction.

It is said that the definition of insanity is doing the same thing repeatedly expecting to get a different result. We've all heard someone with no intention to change the way they do business say, "perhaps if I just try harder next time!" The best question we can ask ourselves then is, *"How?...How can I achieve my desired outcome?"* When we pose this question to our unconscious, AND we are open to the answers, our unconscious can come up with the correct response. Remember, your unconscious mind is your team—keep a good communication going and it will find a way to carry out orders.

If you're having trouble staying on course and persisting in your pursuit of this one goal, perhaps you need to explore how important that end goal really is to you. Ask yourself:

- *Is it something that I really want?*
- *What is important to me about it and what am I willing to do to get it?*
- *How important is it that I achieve this particular goal?*
- *What is the value to me and others of achieving this goal?*
- *What is the cost to me if I quit now and go on a different path?*
- *Is there another end game that is more meaningful to me that would fulfill my highest values?*

In 1998, when I hit a low point in my volleyball career after being dropped again by my playing partner, and by my coaches, I started to question continuing in my quest for the Olympic. I contemplated other paths like settling down on the Gold Coast, getting a regular job, nothing too appealing other than avoiding what seemed a merry-go-round of disappointment after disappointment. In other words, I wasn't very motivated "towards" any new goals in particular, but rather, more "away from" the struggles I was dealing with at the time.

In thinking over my options, I also considered how I might feel in 2000 if I chose to quit, wondering how I would deal with the eternal question, "What if...?" I thought about the cost of *not* pursuing my dream. "Not going for it" was not a real option for me because I didn't have a viable option to replace it. In my case, I chose not to change my course. However, if there is not enough compelling you toward your set goal, shifting direction can be the best choice.

Just remember, you can't just NOT do something. If you decide to end the pursuit of your goal, you do need a replacement goal or dream in order for you to feel truly fulfilled and propelled toward something you care about. Otherwise, you could end up just feeling stuck and directionless.

If you set a new goal, and it is something achievable, continue no matter what. I agree with the creative entrepreneur Walt Disney, who said, *"If you can dream it, you can do it."* I believe we all have the inner resources to do *anything* we set our mind to.

Put Your Practice Into Action

It has been said that, "it takes eight years to be an overnight success." You often only see the end result of other people's success... you need to look a little deeper to see what had to happen before that success could happen. What steps did that person take to get that win?

Each time you take steps forward and dare to fail, you move closer to your end-goal. Even if it is two steps forward and one step back, you are still getting closer to the goal. Once you expand your awareness to new possibilities, you can never go back to your old limitations.

The picture I like best to describe this point is this: imagine pushing something through a small hole in a wall. There is great resistance in getting through this hole, and you may need several attempts to break through. You might even need some help from others to build up enough force to push through the barrier. Once you do push through, the resistance goes away, and you are into a larger room of possibilities.

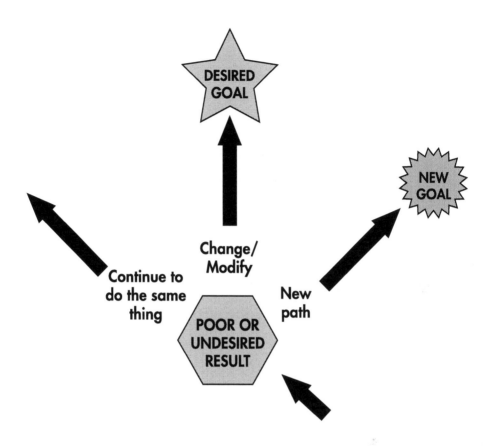

Though at times it seems futile to push through a barrier in your life, once you do, it opens you up to even greater possibilities and greater success, perhaps more than you ever imagined.Now that you are taking a new direction after your sporting career, your path might not yet be clear. That's okay. It may feel like a new start, but it's also just the next step in a lifelong string of successes and games from which you are constantly learning. Just take one step…then another. Move forward in some way towards your idea. Start to do something. Anything!

By taking action towards a goal, you'll be surprised at what opportunities come in your life to make it easier. Remember your

Reticular Activating System is at work to make things a bit easier for you to search for anything in alignment with your ideal picture of the future you have in mind. When those opportunities come, you need to take them—that's the universe passing you the ball or puck or baton…take it and run with it.

Do something everyday towards your goal. Whether you have a clear action plan or not, I suggest you ask yourself everyday, *"What's one action I can take today towards my goal?"* Pose the question to yourself and expect an answer. Perhaps not right away, but by asking the question your unconscious mind will get to work on the problem and provide a solution. Often the answer comes in the form of an idea. Sometimes the answer comes in your dreams. Sometimes it comes in the form of an opportunity presented out of the blue by someone you know or don't know.

It's the little things that you do every single day that will get you to your goal. One step a day is 365 steps a year. That's huge! What do you need to do to start today?

Have a Plan

When I am working with clients in business, I ask them if they have a business plan. Often they do not. You may have heard the saying, "failing to plan is planning to fail." Whether you are in business or not, you can benefit a great deal from having a plan in writing. There are a number of planning tools freely available on the internet and in the "Business" section of bookstores with business plans, time-management systems, quarterly plans, 120-day plans, project plans, and so on. Find a planning system that works for you and start putting your thoughts to paper. Don't wait to have it all thought out before you start writing, or you will never get started. Get the planning document or template and use it to stimulate your thoughts. Write down what comes to mind. You can always change it later. I think of my plans as being organic—alive and adapting to changes.

You can start with a blank piece of paper and draw out the big picture. Where do you want to be in one year, five years or 10 years time? Once you've got the big picture, you can work backwards from there—break down your long-term goal into the steps and details that will get you there. If you want to achieve a certain goal in twelve months time, then consider what you will have to achieve at the ten-month stage to ensure you are on track, and keep backing up month by month to see, what else would you have to do before you could do that? What would you have had to achieve two months prior to that? You can keep working your way back from the future goal until you arrive at where you are right now. This way, you will know exactly what you need to accomplish in this next month, week, and tomorrow for you to arrive at your goal twelve months from now.

A coach or mentor can help you with your planning, whether guiding your thoughts, asking you the right questions, or providing you with the structure and details. It depends on the type of coach you work with. There are coaches who specialize in business plans and strategies.

Trust That Things Are Perfect as They Are

As you move forward each day, there will be many times you may wonder why you are in a certain situation. This is particularly true when those situations are deemed to be negative by most accounts. It is particularly true in those bad times, however, that being able to trust the process can help you immensely. This means trusting that you are in the right place and everything is still falling into place, maybe just not in the way you anticipated.

These are the critical times when you can learn to trust your ability to take on something new. You can acquire the experience and understanding that will enable you to become the person that you want to be.

The ability to trust is a learned skill you have to practice, everyday. When you get to the point where you believe you're in the right place and you've let go of the need to have things go exactly as you want, taking this stance or position can actually help propel your progress forward. This is particularly true if you take the time to look at your current situation. When you're willing to believe there is something good you can learn from anything you are experiencing, you learn more quickly and move on to a solution more easily.

People who start to break down under adversity and don't trust that they are in the right position, can start playing the victim, saying to themselves and others, "Why is this happening to me?!" This stance only contributes to a feeling that you have no control, which makes you more likely to throw up your hands and say, "Why bother?" Your negative feelings actually aggravate the situation, making it true for you because now you really do start to lose control.

It starts with your attitude which projects onto the situation so that's all you can see. You stop seeing opportunities, openings where suddenly the obstacles disappear. That's why you need to believe you're always in the right place even when things seem negative.

Stay resourceful, thinking positively, and start doing the things you *can* do today to move your whole life forward.

SUCCESS TRAINING EXERCISE:
My One-Year Game Plan

· ·

Take the time to write down a game plan to achieve your DREAM goal. This could be a business plan or something less formal. Decide on the planning tool best for you, as described previously. Start with the big picture and add details as they come to you. If you haven't got an official planner yet, you can brainstorm here. Start to set your Game Plan:

What actions do you need to take in order to achieve your ultimate goal?

_____

_____

_____

_____

_____

_____

_____

_____

Where would you like to be in 12 months?

_____

What would need to happen in 10 months for that to be possible?

_____

8 months?

_____

6 months?

_____
_____
_____
_____
_____
_____

4 months?

_____
_____
_____
_____
_____

2 months?

_____
_____
_____
_____
_____

What is something you can do today, or this week to start moving toward your goal?

_____

_____

_____

_____

_____

_____

_____

_____

_____

Summary

✓ Be prepared to do whatever it takes to achieve your goal
✓ When you get to an obstacle, find alternative ways to get to your goal
✓ The more you fail the more you will succeed

A successful person falls down nine times and gets up ten.

COMPETITION DEBRIEF

"It's never too late to be who you might have been."

• George Eliot

Post-Olympic Blues

I finished my Olympic competition on day three after two games of volleyball. The second game against Germany was disappointing, and I felt deflated. I remember thinking, *"Was that all?"* I spent the rest of the Olympic Games watching other competitions, soaking up the atmosphere, and supporting our Australian team in Beach Volleyball. My teammates Kerri Pottharst and Natalie Cook surprised everybody beating Brazil to win Gold. That was incredibly exciting but... my direct involvement was over. My post-Olympic blues had already begun.

I had spent 25 years dreaming of this experience. So much focus, intense effort, and time went into making it to the Olympics. Then, by the third day, my life dream came to an abrupt halt. I was out of the competition. I was just gutted, thinking, *"Is this it?"* After being on such a high at the opening ceremony only three days earlier, it was quite a long way to fall. Having such a high goal had given me purpose and direction for most of my life. What would I do now? Where would I go from here?

The Transition from Sport to "Normal Life"

I decided to leave international competition for good and settle down to have a "normal life." At thirty-four, I had knee and back pain for which I needed regular therapy. The only reason I had kept playing, pushing through the pain, was to achieve the Olympic goal. Now that I had accomplished what I set out to do, I was looking forward to my new, pain-free life. I wouldn't have to train so vigorously, I could go out and socialize, and finally find a special person to share my life with. It was time for some well-deserved rest.

At first, I resisted the easy path of falling back on physiotherapy, as I didn't really enjoy treating people. It was not fulfilling enough for me. Instead, I was looking for something new and challenging, like sports marketing or media. A few good opportunities came along that I enjoyed, including temporary work with the West Australian Institute of Sport, then with the Olympic Council. However, neither had long-term prospects for me. After travelling the world, I had gotten used to a certain kind of lifestyle, so I wanted fulfilling work, but at the same time, I still highly valued flexibility. While I was training and traveling, I didn't place much importance on getting ahead financially. I always believed that I would "get by," and that's exactly what I did—I got by.

I was pretty naïve with regard to investing and continued with my save-whatever-I-can strategy. What was more important to me at the time was having fun, freedom, fulfillment, independence, and variety. Consequently, these all showed up as my experience. I remember thinking that, when it came to exercise, I didn't want to feel like I *had* to do anything. After years of being a disciplined fitness fanatic, I was ready to enjoy some freedom.

Living in Perth during that period, I instead felt lonely and isolated. Though I had dear friends, I had been so used to being part of a team since an early age, I didn't seem to know how to live effectively in a world that didn't involve training, sport, competition, and travel. I didn't have anything to look forward to. That special man who was going to just turn up and marry me when I retired didn't arrive. My friends were married with kids while I was feeling like a teenager wanting to experience life without restrictions. It was a very confusing time for me.

Then, six months after the Sydney games, I had surgery on my right knee. I was experiencing a lot of physical discomfort from the tendonitis I'd suffered for years, and now calcification, small pieces of bone, in my front thigh muscle just above the kneecap were causing me additional pain. I arranged to have the bone removed. To prevent irritation of the muscle post-surgery, I had to wear an orthopaedic brace for four weeks and use crutches. At first, I didn't mind so much. As the weeks wore on, I grew frustrated at how restricted I was trying to get about, making me feel even more isolated and alone. The lack of physical activity made it worse. I couldn't rely on exercise to give me a natural boost of adrenaline. One of the causes of depression is an imbalance in brain chemistry, in particular low serotonin levels. Lack of exercise or activity can contribute to low serotonin. Professional athletes need to be particularly aware of that physical factor influencing their overall sense of well-being.

I entered into a darker part of my life as I focused on the negative aspects of my daily existence, like being alone. I was looking for happiness outside of myself and couldn't find it anywhere. I vividly remember sitting on the couch one day crying and crying and rocking to console myself. After having achieved so much in my life, I felt powerless to do anything. Being as independent-minded as I was then, I didn't think to ask for help. I didn't dare admit to anyone how awful I was feeling. And worse, I couldn't see any possible solution. Despite the fact that I really didn't feel like living, I couldn't see ending my life as a solution either. I still valued the gift of life and always had some strength to know that I needed to work through my pain. Deep down inside, I knew there had to be a better way.

That's when I decided to work for a mentoring organization called Great Mates. A charity supported by the government, Great Mates made use of athletes to mentor and inspire hope for troubled youths. I was involved with helping the group get started in Western Australia, helping to promote and market fundraising activities. The job involved sports marketing and other skills I enjoyed. Plus, I loved mentoring others to make the most of their lives. I got the opportunity to speak to groups, both kids and business groups, about my experiences and started to become more aware of the message I had to deliver. It was ironic that I was inspiring hope in others, while still struggling to find my own hope within. The positive response I received, and the idea that I had so much teach, ignited in me a new growing level of passion.

It was time to make changes for myself. Meanwhile, I had met a man who lived in the eastern states. With the possibility of Great Mates expanding into Queensland, I decided to move back east to my home state once again. I was used to taking risks to follow my dreams and that included taking a risk on love. I was still an unhappy person at that time, vulnerable and willing to do anything to find love. Neither the relationship nor the job eventuated, but I was thankful to be back near my family and friends. I had long lived by the philosophy that things happen for a reason, and being back in Queensland felt right for me. Working with Great Mates gave me the chance to see that I could inspire others, and that felt right too. I would be drawn in that direction again. For now, it was back to job-hunting.

Though I always had the physiotherapy degree to fall back on, I resisted what would've felt like backsliding, now that I knew it was possible to enjoy a fulfilling career. For some reason, I chose a completely different field and got a marketing job with a music website. It was more selling than marketing, and sales was not my strength then, but I thought I could at least learn something new and gain experience. The hours were interesting too. We dealt mainly with the US market, so I started at five in the morning and finished by eleven that same morning. The part-time arrangement still allowed me time for beach volleyball. Volleyball was something I still loved and something I was good at. I decided to prepare for the national tour and picked up a new partner.

My initial intention was to play only the Australian tour in 2001/2002. My partner begged me to return to international competition, and I declined. As the season continued and I started to enjoy playing again, I became more fulfilled by volleyball and less fulfilled with my work. I wasn't doing very well with sales and didn't seem to be learning much. By the end of the season and after injuries to my original partner, I again had a new partner...I was back playing with Nicole Sanderson. She had recovered from her second ACL reconstruction and was eager to get back playing internationally again. Nicole wanted to qualify for 2004 Olympics. Even though this was not my goal, I was playing so well that I decided that I would at least return to international competition. Perhaps I could resolve some unfinished business and create the kind of results I dreamed of, perhaps even make top four.

I loved playing on the World Beach Volleyball Tour in 2002. I had a coach who believed and supported me, and I was playing with a new love for the game. At 36, I was fitter than ever. The highlight that year was finishing 5th at a tournament in Montreal, Canada. I had not achieved such a high finish since my first year on the World Tour in 1994.

Gradually, though, I realized that I did want more out of life than just a volleyball career. I started to get disenchanted with the partnership. Failing to qualify in Brazil, the last tournament of the international season, signaled the end for me. We were knocked out of the qualifier, and I decided I wanted to go home. I even proceeded to change my flights. I managed to get out of Brazil on an earlier flight, but I missed a tight connection and I was caught up in Santiago, Chile, for two nights. I am so grateful for that chance to step out on my own. Those two days and nights ended up being so amazing, they transformed my outlook on life.

I took the time to be spontaneous and explored the beautiful city, enjoying the architecture, the markets, and the gardens. I didn't mind travelling alone and was quite good at enjoying my own company. The snow-capped Andes Mountain that towers over Santiago inspired the adventurer in me, so I found a ski company and booked a trip for the next morning that included a ski lesson. I had skied only once before for a few hours in Austria. I had yet to learn the skill.

This day remains a highlight of my life...going up to the snow in the Andes Mountains for a day; I learned to ski on top of the world. And that's exactly how I felt—I was on top of the world! I continued on from my one-hour lesson to practice and practice, taking in as much skiing as I could in that one magical day. The views were breathtaking, and I took some incredible photographs that continue to inspire me. At the end of the day, I got back on the bus trip home, returned to my hotel, collected my luggage, and went immediately to the airport for the flight back to Australia.

In that one day, I learned how joyful life can be when you go with the flow. I developed a better appreciation of what is now of value in my life—to enjoy the moment, be present and experience adventure. At the end of the Australian summer, I decided to retire from national beach volleyball and focus once again on working and settling down—this time around, I was ready to enjoy the ride.

It continued to be a bumpy ride, yet I was overall in a better place emotionally. I once again had a variety of jobs that were all great experiences and eventually contributed to a rich platform on which I based my current success. I developed experience in sales, speaking, working with school-kids, and event management. I was still not getting ahead financially, and so by mid-2003 I made the decision to go back to physiotherapy, something I trusted and knew would help me earn some decent money. I picked up a part-time clinical job, and I also got a second part-time job in Corporate Health. At that time it was a dream job for me because it utilized my knowledge of physiotherapy as well as general health and fitness, while incorporating my skills in speaking and coaching. I loved it because it was about health and injury prevention, so I could encourage others to look after themselves. It was my first step towards helping others make important behavioral changes, which is largely what I do now in my own business.

For a while, I then combined clinical work with the corporate health work. It seemed to be a habit of mine, combining part-time jobs rather than committing to full-time positions, to give me some freedom, which I had enjoyed throughout my volleyball career. Eventually, the work with corporate health grew, and I took that on full-time. My role expanded also as the company grew in Queensland, taking on more employees. I became a state operations manager overseeing a small team that grew to four. When the national sales manager left, I put my hand up for that too. I had gained experience in sales since my days with the music website and was accepted for the role. My life was pretty full, and I was content.

Throughout this period I still often fell back into volleyball as a comfort zone. It was an area where I could be competitive and successful. When I was on the court, I still had a ferocious desire to win. I remember a comeback season in 2005, at age 39, when I started playing on the Queensland state tour with a friend just to have fun. We played the first tournament with little preparation and despite being the twelfth seeds, came through and won the final. We were not particularly attached to the outcome and played without a care, which is a great way to play.

As I played, I demonstrated that I still had the fitness and the abilities at the top level, which came to the attention of Natalie Cook. Cook was in need of a temporary partner for the summer. She was now playing with Nicole Sanderson, who was missing the season with shoulder problems. I was elated to have the opportunity to play on the National Tour competitively and worked hard to get into the fittest shape I had even been. Just a few weeks short of my fortieth birthday, Cook and I made a final on the National Tour. We didn't get to win a title, but I also managed two more third placings that season too. Volleyball was still a big part of who I was. Though I was trying to make finances and stability more important to me, fun and competition were still in the top three values that showed up in my life.

Turning Point

I consider the years between 2000 and 2006 my transition years. By 2006 I was doing well, but things were only okay. I had a satisfying job, I had a boyfriend, I owned a home...I was realizing my dream of being "normal." However, now I wanted more. I started to get glimpses that perhaps I could do more. I went to my first weekend-long seminar. It was the first time that I invested in my own learning and personal development beyond books. I had come to realize that even though I was reading books and thought I knew what to do, the fact was that I wasn't doing it. I wasn't creating the results I truly wanted in my life.

The weekend in May 2006 that I went to a fire-walking event run by Kurek Ashley, called "The Fire Within," woke me up. It did in fact stir the fire within, the passion that had gone out with the Sydney Olympics closing ceremony had been relit inside me. I decided then that I needed to lift my game and expect more out of life. I didn't know how, and I didn't know what, but walking across that fire made me see that I was capable of much more than I thought. What I also realized was that *I* was responsible for making it happen and more importantly, that I was responsible for my own happiness. From that weekend, I stopped looking outside of myself for happiness and discovered some inner contentment.

I didn't recreate my life overnight. It was a start. A few months later a friend invited me to another course...Chris Howard's "Breakthrough to Success." Initially I was excited by the opportunity for further learning, then as the weekend came around I started to lose interest. I questioned devoting a whole weekend to what I thought would be "more of the same stuff!" "Didn't I know it already?" I questioned. Luckily I ignored my doubts and went anyway to see what it was all about. I'm glad I did because I was hooked from the first five minutes. If Kurek had stirred me to what was possible for me, Chris Howard showed me the path.

Fascinated with how the mind influences our behaviors and results, I wanted to know more. I wanted to learn the tools and techniques so that I too could empower others. I wanted to become a coach and teacher. I was committed now to creating a new life for myself—I made the decision and signed up for further study, more excited than I had been in a long time to put this training into action.

For the first time, since September 2000, I had a major goal and direction to move towards. I had the strength to believe in myself and set powerful intentions for my future. I realized I could still win Gold. It was no longer the Olympic medal I was interested in...I could fulfill what was truly important to me and go for the real gold in life. I stepped into my own power and knew that I would be teaching this valuable information to others within a year or two. I knew that I too would be on a platform speaking to hundreds of people, inspiring them to believe in their own dreams. I knew that this time it would not be a lie, that I would be walking the talk 100%.

I finally committed to making the transition from sportsperson to businessperson. I still played volleyball that summer of 2006-2007 on both the state and national tour. It was a chance to put my new skills to practice. I had taken my first course of study to become a Results Coach and NLP Practitioner, working with the mindset to achieve results. I worked on both myself and my fellow players and enjoyed seeing the positive changes in both.

By the end of the season, my passion for volleyball had dwindled so that I couldn't even make myself play the final tournament of the season. I had deliberately changed my values and beliefs so much that it affected how I spent my time and energy. I shifted to placing more importance now on my career and started my own business. For the first time in my life, I felt like I had nothing more to prove out on the court. I felt like I could say good-bye to competitive volleyball for good. I retired for the third and last time for the right reasons—I was finally moving *towards* something new and exciting.

I could now put 100% of my focus on my business, Annetteffect, training to become a Master coach and trainer of NLP. I also moved more time and attention onto creating greater wealth in my life and, as it happens, that grew too. Up until then I had been content with just getting by. Now I wanted to create more in my life, to enjoy an easier lifestyle, to travel again and to make a difference in the world.

Though I was making changes and had exciting new goals, my self-perception was slow to change. As I had my whole life, I still saw myself as a sportsperson. Even though I was doing the right things to create a business, I didn't yet see myself as a "business-person." Because I was good at sport, I limited myself to thinking that was *all* I was good at. I had worked to change my beliefs and values, and had a new approach to life, however, I was still missing one thing...the realization that I was much more than I even knew. I had to expand my mindset even more to see that I had an even greater identity and grander purpose.

. . . .

WINNING POINT #8:
Expand Your Identity

"Too many people make the past their identity and spend the rest of their lives accumulating sympathy for their past pain."

• Dr. Laura Schlessinger

The Winner's Edge

How you identify yourself has an overarching kind of control over everything you do. Your identity will influence your beliefs and values and even your goals and aspirations. So many aspects of my life fell into place more easily once I defined myself in a new way as an entrepreneur and Coach. It broadened my possibilities and gave me so much direction and momentum, I accomplished more in a shorter period of time. I recognized that I could be and do whatever I chose to, and still use all the skills and abilities I had acquired along the way in sport.

All too often, people limit themselves by putting a label on who they are or what they do. A person may identify with their job, their hobby, interests, lineage, race, gender, or even their emotions; eg) "I am depressed." You can gain insight into your identity as well as others through their "I am…" statements and a person can have several. "I am a great success…I am a failure…I am aggressive…I am a bad negotiator…etc."Identity is often attached to actions or past incidents. For example, having made a mistake, a person might identify with being bad, or a loser, rather than limiting the label to the action or result alone. Instead of saying, "that was a bad move," "that was an ineffective action," they'll tell themselves, "I am a failure." People, in general, can be far more likely to dwell on errors, losses and missed chances in life, letting those gradually change their self-perception for the worse. Athletes, perhaps, run the risk even more of allowing themselves to be defined by notorious game losses, rather than focusing on all the wins and amazing things we have accomplished. Learning to define yourself anew on your own terms gives you the winner's edge in everything you do. It just requires some mental flexibility.

Be Mentally Fit and Flexible

It is important to understand your current identity. To recreate yourself, in a sense, can be the difference between being attached to your past results as an athlete, and dragging them with you into your future, or moving on successfully with a new expanded and well-rounded identity. Humans have a basic need for importance and significance. Unfortunately, this sense is often lost during retirement from sport. A sporting career produces many regular rewards and near constant feedback—these are not often found in everyday life outside of sport. That's why it's so important that you provide a way to recognize and improve yourself on your own, or find coaches who can support you.

Change is always possible at all times and in all areas. This book, and my work as a coach now, is all about making changes in your way of thinking, and, thereby, changing your results. To give you a clearer understanding of how we are changing all the time, and how *you* can direct change to your advantage, let me break down for you the hierarchy of change—*how* we change.

How We Change

Real change occurs first at the unconscious level, beyond conscious thought. Internal and external changes occur naturally throughout our sport careers and beyond. They can come as a direct result of our effort, in the same way our training changes our performance; or they can occur subtly over time, unscheduled and beneath the surface of our awareness in varying degrees.

There is a suggested hierarchy in levels that cause change, based on the work of anthropologist, Gregory Bateson. Change at certain levels of thinking can be more effective than others where the highest level causes the deepest and longest-lasting change.

1. At the lowest level, you can change your **Environment** by a change of location and/or change the people with whom you associate but you will essentially remain unchanged.

2. Changing **Behavior** can produce greater change. When you retrain your body to change a bad habit on the court by doing drills, for example, you are directly changing a behavior. .

3. When you learn new skills and increase your overall **Capabilities** it becomes easy and part of who you are. Being capable means you no longer have to think about your new ability consciously.

4. Changing your **Beliefs** will alter what you are capable of and therefore you will behave differently. This is a more significant change to make, as it has a ripple effect into those other levels. For example, if you believe you can earn one million dollars, then you will display different behaviors/actions and abilities then if you were to believe, "I will always be poor," or "I'm not good at making money."

5. Since **Values** are what are important to you and serve to motivate you, then it makes sense that changing your values will

WINNING POINT #8: EXPAND YOUR IDENTITY   221

change how your run your life. If you introduce the value of 'Love' into your top 5 values then you will start behaving differently, and you will have new beliefs about life, career and relationships.

6. Making a change at the level of **Identity** is the most effective for long-lasting change, affecting all other levels of values, beliefs, abilities, behaviors, and environment.

Change created at a higher level of thought creates change to levels below it

    Identity
       →Values
          →Beliefs
             →Capabilities
                →Behavior
                   →Environment

Forming Your New Identity

You see how this works—I moved around often over the years, changing partners, and locations, but those surface changes didn't affect my more deeply-rooted values and beliefs; therefore, very little changed for me in terms of my results. I mistakenly thought that those environmental changes would make a bigger difference for me and get me closer to my goal. Later on, as I was trying to make the transition into a new career from sport, I realized how strongly my identity was still wrapped up in my sporting past...it made more sense to me why I continued to struggle to move on and start over. By creating a change at this highest level of the hierarchy, more substantial change was then possible throughout the other levels.

A change at the level of identity will completely transform your life. This constitutes a lot of the work that I do with clients who are either struggling to make a transition or choice in their life, or taking on new skills and abilities—we go in and do the change at both the conscious and unconscious levels of values, beliefs and identity. This provides the most direct path to their end goals, effectively creating long-term change with the least amount of effort.

Here's another fantastic example of the power of identity—Australian beach volleyball players, Natalie Cook and Kerri Pottharst, purposefully started to identify themselves as Olympic Gold Medalists a full eighteen months before going to the Sydney Games in 2000 where they won Gold. They didn't wait to have the proof before starting to *behave* like gold medalists. They saw themselves as *already being* that which they wanted to become.

Be-Do-Have

Identity is about who you are "being" inside. What you *do* and *have* in life comes from there. Often people will wait to *be* someone or something thinking they have to do something or have something in their possession first. For example, "I'll be happy when I have…" or "I'll be successful when I do…." Most people operate in life from a Have-Do-Be principle. They keep putting off success or even doing the things they would do once they have that job, that amount of money, that car, etc.

The secret is to be whatever it is you want to be right now, even if that means acting *as if* you are already that. Let's talk about being charitable. Is that something you put off until you have enough money? Most wealthy people got in the habit of being charitable while they were still poor. There is much written on the 10% rule, including the parable "The Richest Man in Babylon" that the only path to riches is through giving – even when you think you have nothing to give.

It's the Be-Do-Have principle. Be and Act as a successful or wealthy person would in order to have. Be happy now to create the results you want. Be a business person now to create success in business. Your actions and possessions will change in accordance with your being and self-identify.

Depending on your current self-identification, you may need to re-evaluate, let go of some of those old self-perceptions that have built up over the years, so that you can start clean a new career. Start to think about it:

- *Who and what do you identify with?*
- *Do you identify with your past, your sport, with being an athlete, a competitor or have you moved on to a new identity?*
- *How would you behave or act if you did have a more desired or appropriate identity?*
- *When you were competing or playing sport, did you identify yourself as being a winner? Or as struggling?*
- *What type of identity would you have to take on in order to get the results you want now out of life?*

It is important to understand your identity as it can be the difference between attaching to your past results as an athlete or to moving on successfully with a new expanded and well-rounded identity.

To re-create success in a new career requires an individual to identify with their new role so that their beliefs, values and actions are all congruent to produce the results they want. Who do you need to BE now to create your success beyond sport?

SUCCESS TRAINING EXERCISE:
Find Your Inner Winner and
Cross-Train Your Skills

• •

Here is a simple writing exercise that will stimulate whatever change needs to occur for you to move forward. It can assist you to make your new identity as certain in your mind as your old identity as an athlete is or was. Your identity might be deeply in-grained, and it can only change as much as you want it to change. The impetus to change comes when you finally recognize just how much your old identity is costing you, and better yet...what a new empowering identity will allow you to do!

Step 1: What is Your Current Identity?

Let's start by creating some awareness around your current identity to see how that has been affecting your results. What are your "I AM" statements? What do you tell yourself at some level? It might be a title (world champion), an occupation or role (mother), or it might be an emotion (angry). You will have several so take the time now to write them all down. But don't think about it for too long; just write whatever comes off the top of your head:

I AM _____

I AM _____

I AM _____

I AM _____

I AM _____

I AM _____

I AM _____

I AM _____

I AM _____

I AM _____

Now, put a ✔ next to the statements that you feel empower you and drive you forward.

Put an **X** next to the statements that you feel disempower you and hold you back.

Step 2: Modeling

I discussed the importance of role models and modeling when working with values. Look at your role model and think of how are they as people. What do you think is their self-identity? What identity must they have in order to create the results they have? Write down some new statements of the type of person you need to be to do in order to accomplish what you want to do.

Examples: I am successful; I am an entrepreneur; I am wealthy; I am joyful.

I AM _____

I AM _____

I AM _____

I AM _____

I AM _____

Note how it is in the present tense, just like our goals. In the *Power of Awareness*, Neville writes of "living in the moment of the wish fulfilled." It is a beautiful and effective concept, to be in the emotional state that you will be in, having already achieved your goal. When you add to that a deeper sense of identity, it is a powerful engine that will drive you towards your goals.

Step 3: Feel Your New Identity

Take a moment now to "try on" and incorporate your new I AM statements within "who you are being." One at a time, sit quietly and feel the feeling of being that "I AM...." See the pictures that come to mind when you're being that I AM.

- *How will I act?*
- *What will I be doing?*
- *How will I feel?*
- *What will I have as this new identity?*

Spend a minute with each, feeling the essence of being.

You may want to put your "I AM" statements on the wall or somewhere you will see it to remind you of who you have chosen to be now. Some people put them on their computer screensavers. Be aware of how it changes your feelings and behaviors. When an old disempowering habit arises, reaffirm what your new identity is and act accordingly.

A note on taking on a new statement such as "I AM WEALTHY"— when you research wealthy people you will find that they are wise with their money and often do not buy into consumerism. That is, they don't go spending their money just because they can. They are wealthy because they don't overspend, or they invest it in commodities they believe will appreciate. I mention this because I don't want you taking on a false notion that you have money to burn, and lose all good sense. Remain wise with what you have. Allow the new identity to lead you toward positively successful new behaviors and habits.

Cross-Train Your Skills

Here's the second part of this Success Exercise. Now that you are identifying with the person you are to become, it's time to cross-train your skills—most, if not all, of the gifts and abilities you possess that contributed to your success in sport can be applied to make your new life a success too. Imagine walking around with the certainty that, "I am as good at sales (or business or my new career) as I was at sport."

When I did this exercise, a very bright light-bulb went off in my head. In a very short space of time, maybe 15 to 30 minutes, I switched from being firmly identified with being a sportsperson to seeing myself as a businessperson. I mapped over all the skills and traits I had as a beach volleyball player to that of being a businessperson. I was shocked at how similar they were. I had been fooling myself to think that I couldn't be successful in a new career.

The idea of this exercise is for you to realize that you already have all the skills and traits that you need within you to be successful at anything you set your mind to. When you get this, you can go out and follow your new path with the certainty and excitement you had when you played your sport. It's time to let go of the old you so a new identity can form and determine your future. Let go of your past, including not only your alleged "failures," but even the successes. Look forward to how you can create success anew. The past is there for you to learn from and not to dwell in.

So here's the last step in the process of transforming your self-perception, and identity. Cross-training your skills means you retain all your current abilities and utilize them to create success beyond sport:

1. What are you currently good at? For example, I strongly identified with being a good beach volleyball player.

_____

_____

_____

_____

_____

2. What would you like to be good at?

_____

_____

_____

_____

3. Write down all the ways that doing Answer 2 is like doing Answer 1?

For example, I wrote down all the ways that having a business is like playing Beach Volleyball. I wrote down things like: "it's tactical, you need to think 2-3 steps ahead, it's aggressive, etc." Commit to spending at least twenty minutes on this exercise. When you think you can't write any more keep thinking...this is when your mind really starts to pop. That's when you get it! The change is already taking root...go!

_____

_____

_____

_____

Summary

✓ Let go of the past and be present to the now and the future possibilities.

✓ Decide who you want to be and how you are showing up

✓ Be aware of your "I am" statements and create an empowering identity

You can be, do, have anything when you put your mind to it

• • CHAPTER EIGHT • •

PODIUM FINISH

"What we call the beginning is often the end. And to make an end is to make a beginning. The end is where we start from."

• T.S. Eliot

In 2006 I had written on a piece of paper a list of desires that I wanted to achieve in my life, highlighting those that were most important to me. These included travelling to Machu Picchu in Peru, going on safari in Africa, travelling overseas one or two times per year, living on an island, owning a home by the sea, being married. The next year I added to my wish list that I wanted to have a home in Hawaii.

By the end of 2007 I had travelled overseas a total of four times for both work and adventure. I had visited Peru and Machu Picchu, and I went to South Africa spending a couple of days at Shamwari Game Reserve.

With an expanded sense of who I was and new set of values, I was getting a clearer picture of how I wanted my life to be. I knew that I wanted to make a difference in this world, though specifically how would shape itself over the coming years. I observed how athletes, current and retired, were making a mess of their lives outside of sport and getting media attention for all the wrong reasons.

I surmised that if these athletes placed greater value on their own character, and took responsibility for their actions that they might act differently. I became passionate about teaching what I knew and helping athletes in the more affected sporting codes such as football and basketball. I also reflected my own sporting career and how my results would have been, had I had this information. If only I knew then what I know now! It was a bit late for my sporting career but not too late for those competing now and in the future.

I was presenting workshops, coaching a few sporting individuals and teams, as well as working with everyday people. Everyone could benefit from applying the champion mindset to his or her own career and life. As well as building my own business, through 2007 and 2008 I was stepping up within the ranks of the organisation that I had trained and studied with - Chris Howard Training. Not only a coach for them, I was also being trained to teach their courses in Australia and around the world.

I had a career that I absolutely loved and that ensured regular international travel and by 2008 the final piece in my dream life came together.

I had made so many changes in my professional life, and in the process I was also changing on a personal level. Some of my friends commented on the change they saw in me – more grounded, more giving. For me, I felt less needy and more involved in the friendships for what I could give. I didn't feel I needed to get anything. I was also creating new networks of friends that I felt even more connected with and that supported my new career, lifestyle and mindset.

I was still looking for Mr Right and had worked a lot on myself in this regard – exploring my beliefs and habits to see what was holding me back in this area of my life. "Why was I, at 42 years old, still single?" It was a question I had been asked a lot by men. It was March 2008 when I finally figured it out.

At that time I had had a crush on someone, and when I didn't get the affection returned I felt rejected and "not good enough." My huge epiphany was when I realised that I actually deserved *better* than this man. That *he* was not good enough for *me*. You see, I had determined what my ideal man was, but I also didn't believe he existed. This had created inner conflict within my mind and sabotaged any progress towards finding a man. In fact I was always compromising.

I rewrote my list of qualities for my ideal man and the relationship, and most important was, that *he* would support my career and be okay with my frequent travel and absences. I could have a great relationship and an amazing career. He would also be into learning and growing, enjoy wine, travel and good food. I opened myself up to the help of the universe and the internet. I had used internet dating with moderate success in the past. This time I decided to include international possibilities and found a site that had an excellent profiling system. Great – I could be specific in what I was looking for.

In the past I had limited what I wrote as I didn't want to minimize my chances of finding someone. This time I didn't want to waste my time on anything less than my ideal man, and therefore the more specific the better. I knew he was out there.

Looking back, even though I teach this stuff, I'm still amazed at how quickly and easily I found him by following this path. Steven was the very first guy to pop up as a likely match, and he was the first person to write to me. There were a couple of others that I exchanged emails with, but Steven was the one who endured beyond the emails to a phone conversation. He lived in Maui, Hawaii, so our relationship would remain long-distance for a couple of months. What a fabulous way to get to know someone – by talking. We met online in May 2008, and I was already in love before I visited him a couple of months later in July.

As of May 2009, I am spending most of my time in Hawaii

living with an amazing man. He is different from what I had previously dated and how happy I am of that. I am grateful for his support and also how he challenges me to grow in different ways than I could ever imagine. Back to the end of 2006 when I had envisioned my future, I had seen myself running along the beach with my man and two dogs, white Labradors. Less than two years later, I was running along a beach in Maui with Steven and his two dogs – black Labradors. Close enough!

• •

MATCH POINT:
Fine Tuning

"First say to yourself what you would be; and then do what you have to do."

• Epictetus

Higher Goals, Bigger Wins

You may notice that once you take on a larger self-identity, your goals grow along with you as a result. So you have to also think beyond the goals you previously set for yourself to what your goals *allow you to do.* A goal itself is not the be-all-end-all. A goal always serves a higher purpose or value. For most of my life, I strove to be an Olympian, never giving one thought to what the next step would be. At the time, I didn't consider that there was a higher purpose for me achieving that goal. Consequently, after the Games were over, I felt lost for awhile. I had never stopped to think, "Going to the Olympics will allow me to do what?"

Now, when you think about each of the goals you set for yourself earlier, consider that there is something greater behind the attainment of that goal. This makes your accomplishment far more meaningful when you get there. When my coaching clients set goals with me for their new career, I always ask the question, "For what purpose? What else will you get from achieving that goal?" You may ultimately use the achievement of your goal to make a difference in the world, or to inspire others or to support a family. When you are motivated towards a higher achievement or benefit beyond the goal itself, it is almost a surety that you are going to achieve your goal.

I believe the universe conspires in favor of those who are looking at goals outside of themselves and looking to help others.

Think a step or two ahead...then when you achieve your intended goal, you can celebrate and appreciate it that much more, as you continue onto the next vision. It is all integrated, and generating a greater purpose for your life.

New Resources, Skills, And Mentors

"All of the top achievers I know are life-long learners... looking for new skills, insights, and ideas. If they're not learning, they're not growing... not moving toward excellence."

• Denis Waitley

I believe in perpetual growth and expansion. I am always seeking what else I can learn to enhance my life. A seminar on personal development and wealth creation changed my thinking and habits around finances and gave me the foundation on which to build additional skills. When you decide to seek more knowledge and skills, you will find that the more you know, the more you realize how much you don't know. A hunger for learning will drive you forward causing you to grow exponentially.

There are many resources, skills, and mentors you have acquired along your journey in sport. Some are obvious to how they can benefit you in other careers, and some are less obvious. Many of you will need to develop new skills and hone them just like you did with the skills of your sport. You have proven you can apply yourself, and it's just a matter of applying yourself anew. As your goals change and grow, you will likely discover that you already have the mindset and many of the skills it takes to accomplish those goals...it also may require that you grow your skill set. As you think about the goals you set for yourself at the start of this book, and the new identity you've just chosen to take on, I want you to identify what resources and skills you may need to achieve them.

When I first retired from sport in 2000, instead of forging a whole career based on my physiotherapy degree, I decided to learn some new skills and did some computer courses to become more familiar with Office software and tools. I explored other interests I enjoyed, like writing and journalism, completing a Diploma in Freelance Journalism in 2001. I pursued a Certificate as a Pilates instructor so I could instruct clients how to take care of themselves, rather than having to treat them.

In addition to getting certified to work with Christopher Howard as a trainer and teach his Results Technologies™ and Neuro-linguistic Programming, I studied internet marketing, multi-level marketing, sales techniques, investing strategies, tele-seminar training, and presentation skills. For me, developing all these new skills has a two-fold benefit—I can apply the skills to use in my own business and life, plus I have a greater knowledge-base to share with my clients. For example, my study and practice of various time-management systems allows me to share the knowledge with clients who are struggling with completing projects, being overwhelmed, prioritizing and finding time to "do it all." I say this to encourage you to pursue your interests, and seek out all the knowledge that's available to you.

You can expand into any field or endeavor you want. If you are letting your past level of education stop you from pursuing further study, then consider that a "limiting belief" and get rid of it! There are many successful people without a formal education or degree. Most notably Richard Branson, who dropped out of high school to head his own company which eventually became Virgin Group. According to Forbes Magazine's 2008 list of billionaires, Branson is listed as having an estimated net worth of approximately $4.4 billion USD.

If you do feel you need a degree or further qualifications to pursue your dream career, then do whatever it takes to get it. If you need to do some pre-qualifying courses, then do them. There are courses and seminars out there for anything and everything you could possibly have a desire to learn. And if it's going to take you ten years of study to achieve your biggest dreams, then do that. You have got to do something in that ten years so you might as well do something fulfilling. It's better to be pointed in the right direction, than wasting those years settling for something less because it was "easy" or you considered it your "only option." Set your sights higher and go for it!

You didn't get where you did in sport by it being easy. You applied yourself, learned new skills and then practised and practised. Perhaps it felt easy to you because you enjoyed it. When you find a course of study that is line with your dream and passion, you will enjoy that too, and then learning will become easier also. I have provided some recommended skills, resources and reading to help you move in the right direction to discover that there is more for you in your future than you may currently realize.

The following are resources or skills many athletes already have:

- Persistence
- Ability to focus
- Teamwork
- Problem solving
- Goal setting

The following are skills you may have in some degree but may need to strengthen:

- Organization
- Time management
- Leadership

The following are key skills to success in any career that are not commonly associated with sport:

- Financial literacy
- Specific career skills
- Networking
- Communication
- Internet
- Sales

Consider now what skills would be useful for you to learn more about to get to your end game; put a check mark next to them and include them in your Game Plan. I've given a few suggestions and left some blank lines for more.

Financial management   ☐
Leadership   ☐
Time Management   ☐
Computer skills   ☐
Internet Marketing   ☐
Marketing   ☐
Networking   ☐
Communication   ☐
Sales   ☐
Investment   ☐
Specific career skills/other ☐

_____

_____

List classes, mentors and resources that could help you integrate these new skills:

_____

_____

_____

_____

_____

_____

_____

_____

Study and Model

In addition to attending courses or seminars to upgrade your skills, keep yourself up to date on current knowledge of your new endeavors. There is no shortage of books and websites, forums and blogs on any topic that you want to know more about. I usually have a few books with me on the go and am already seeking my next read before I've finished what I have. I have created a list here that I hope you find useful to learn more about some of the specific skills I have mentioned. Here is my recommended reading list to study and model whatever works for you. I consider these as "must-reads" for anyone pursuing his or her own personal and professional development:

TIME MANAGEMENT
7 Habits of Highly Effective People - Steven R. Covey
The One-Minute Manager – Ken Blanchard

LEADERSHIP
How to Win Friends and Influence People – Dale Carnegie
Winning – Jack Welch
The Leadership Pill – Ken Blanchard

FINANCE / WEALTH
Think and Grow Rich – Napolean Hill
Turning Passions into Profits – Chris Howard
How to Make One Hell of a Profit and Still Go to Heaven – Dr. John DeMartini
Rich Dad Poor Dad – Robert Kiyosaki
Rich Woman – Kim Kiyosaki
Secrets of the Millionaire Mind – T. Harv Eker
The Richest Man in Babylon – George Samuel Clason

GOAL ACHIEVEMENT/BUSINESS

Maximum Achievement: Strategies and Skills that Will Unlock your Hidden Powers to Succeed – Brian Tracey
Power of Focus – Jack Canfield
E-myth – Michael E. Gerber

BIOGRAPHIES

Losing my Virginity – Richard Branson
The Way of the Shark – Greg Norman

SALES

The Ultimate Cash Machine – Chet Holmes
Persuasion: The Art of Getting What You Want – Dave Lakhani
Persuasion: They Psychology of Influence – Robert Cialdini

SPIRITUAL DEVELOPMENT

Conversations with God – Neale Donald Walshe
Dynamic Laws of Prosperity – Catherine Ponder
The Divine Matrix – Greg Bradden
The Answer – John Assaraf and Murray Smith
Ask and It is Given: Learning to Manifest your Desires – Esther Hicks
The Power of Now – Eckhart Tolle
The Pilgrimage – Paulo Coelho

Celebrate Along The Way

"The more you praise and celebrate your life, the more there is in life to celebrate."

• Oprah Winfrey

As you start to achieve some milestones, it's important to acknowledge each achievement. You may not get as much outside recognition as you once did in sport. There are fewer glory moments when the crowd is buoying you up and celebrating your wins. You have to take the time to recognize that you are doing positive things, taking steps towards your larger goals. Celebrate every step along the way. You know how good you feel when someone else acknowledges something you have done well—it spurs you on to do even better. Compare that to someone who always puts you down. I know some people that are very good at putting themselves down, looking at what they haven't done or achieved. Why not focus on what you have achieved. Be your own best raving fan. It serves the same purpose, keeping you motivated and pumped up over the journey.

Throughout this book I've spoken about your unconscious mind and its influence on your results. I've related it to being the team-members of a team all working together to produce the result desired of the captain or coach, your conscious mind. When the team members are doing something good, you want to reward them and praise them, "Well done!!" Give them a pat on the back and confirm that you are on track towards what you want and what makes you happy.

I know as an athlete, I often was looking ahead to the next challenge and didn't stop to think about what I had accomplished. It took me years to acknowledge the success I had created in becoming an Olympian. Having achieved that goal, at the time, I was already looking forward and thinking, *"What next?"* I think most athletes can relate.

My poor unconscious mind, my inner team, must have been thinking, "Boy, what do we need to do to make her happy??" Perhaps they may have even started wondering whether it was worth "working" so hard for me at all. Where was the reward in all the hard work?!

Don't make the same mistake. Celebrate every small achievement. It doesn't have to be a party or anything big. You could simply do a little victory dance after pulling off a great interview, or a loud cheer—"Woo-hoooo! I am incredible! I rock!"—and a nice dinner at your favorite restaurant for securing some seed money for your new venture. Whatever it is for you, just make sure you do something for yourself as nice as you would for someone else who supported you or did a lot of work for you. Some clients of mine reward themselves with gifts, though I would reserve this for larger achievements, otherwise it could get costly with all you'll be accomplishing each week.

Share your celebration with friends, and announce to the world that you are a success and making things happen right now.

Game On!

Congratulations on getting this far. If you worked diligently through the exercises, you will be feeling somewhat different about yourself and your life already. The progress has only just begun! You will have some new goals, a greater belief in yourself and a new path, and perhaps you will be living life from a new set of values and identity. Keep this book handy to refer to and even repeat the exercises as needed. Your life will be constantly changing and adapting, and your responses in the future may be different from those you're creating now. Challenge yourself to continue to grow.

I encourage you to seek out further learning of both knowledge of yourself. I am constantly reassessing where I am in the present and where I am going in the future. It makes for an exciting journey when you realize all that you have created already and how much more you can do when you set your mind to it.

My feelings and emotions are what keep me on track. They guide me to recognize whether I'm making good or bad decisions, alert me to any problems, and spur me on to do something about them. I work at being my own best coach, and so should you. I don't always get it right, but that's when my Coach helps me along to climb greater heights or even just to reach my goals quicker.

It's your turn now to set a new clear path, then get out there and play hard. Good luck and remember when you reach your next goal, it's time to reset again. *Where do you want to go? What do you want the final score to be? How would you like your life to be measured? What do you want your fans to say about you?*

The further you dig into your thoughts and unconscious mind, the more you will find and the further there is to dig. Do not despair that you keep coming up against new challenges. Instead, get excited...the process of being a great success is the same as the way diamonds are formed. I have some clients who are upset when a particular moment of their history keeps coming up with lessons for them to learn. They figure they had already dealt with that episode of their past. Get excited because the more you learn the more you will grow. Think of a skyscraper building—the higher the building the deeper the foundation you will need.

How high do you want to go? It's your choice...

MY HALL OF CHAMPIONS

• • ACKNOWLEDGEMENTS • •

Being a first time author there were many people involved in getting his book into print, some directly and some as inspiration for both the book and my journey. Here are the champions that had the greatest impact.

This book, and various concepts of it, has been an idea in my mind since participating in the Olympic Games in 2000. Towards the end of 2008 I was drawn towards helping retired athletes transform their own lives, as I did mine. Once I decided this, I have my strategic coach at the time, Kelly O'Neill to thank for giving me the kick I needed as well as the clarity to complete this book

The inspiration for my own transformation and effective transition is attributed to the magnificence of Chris Howard, my teacher, mentor, employer and friend. His teachings have influenced me and the methods I use in my coaching and programs and I greatly appreciate his support in sharing this with you. I am indebted to Chris for his personal advice in my career development, and the opportunities presented to me through both working with the Christopher Howard Companies and my involvement with the Billionaire Adventure Club.

Big thanks to Aricia Lee, my editor, who helped craft my words and coordinated the book into something easy for athletes and others to read and benefit from. Her encouragement and belief that this was a book that needed to be published was key to me pushing through the challenges. Aricia's contribution, beyond the writing process, was above and beyond my expectations, in advice and support.

Once I decided that self-publishing was my best option I brought Lynne Klippel and Love your Life publishing on board to assist the process. Lynne made my publishing experience so much easier than I could have imagined. The investment has been doubly returned, and I thank Lynne for the peace of mind that I knew this book would succeed, just as the message it delivers.

Bronwyn Boyle has been generous in her support of material on the Olympian Archetype, included at the beginning of the book. Her knowledge on archetypes is extensive and when I heard her describe the experiences of the Olympian Archetype, and how I could relate to the experience, I knew this was a vital link for this book. I am so appreciative of Bronwyn's continued support.

I would like to thank my beach volleyball colleagues, 2000 Olympic Gold Medallists, Kerri Pottharst and Natalie Cook, first for their inspiration in demonstrating what it takes to pursue the ultimate dream and the power of self-belief. Both are dear friends and have provided encouragements of my new career and this book, providing connections, advice and help wherever possible. They are amazing champions.

My dearly loved sister, Katrina Vuori, is amazing for her unwavering support and encouragement for all that I have done and am yet to do. I know I can always count on her, and the time we spend together is always cherished.

Thanks to my Dad for his love, support and blessing throughout my sporting career and beyond. I know it was a roller-coaster ride of emotion and I appreciate him being there for the ups and downs. I would also like to thank his partner, Nora, for her contribution the past 10 years.

I cannot complete this acknowledgement without extending

my heartfelt thanks to my boyfriend and partner in life, Steven Lynch. As well as his contribution to proof-reading and editing, his emotional support has been rock-fast in guiding me through the challenge of stepping into a higher game.

There are many more that have been a source of support and encouragement, too many to single out a few; from my colleagues and fellow coaches to my closest friends. You know who you are – I thank you greatly.

With gratitude,
Annette

ABOUT THE AUTHOR

Annette Huygens-Tholen is a distinguished athlete who represented Australia for 15 years in Indoor and Beach Volleyball. In 2000, she was a proud participant in the Olympic Games in Sydney, achieving one of her life-long goals.

On her initial retirement from sport, Annette worked in sport management with the West Australian Institute of Sport, the WA Olympic Council, and toured Queensland schools speaking to students with the Get Active Schools Program. Using her education in physiotherapy, Annette then found her niche in corporate health, fulfilling her passion to help people help themselves rather than treating them.

An avid reader, Annette's interest in personal, and later spiritual, development began in the mid 1990's. In 2006, she started attending seminars to improve her life and realized that there was more to achieve beyond her sporting success. Annette's focus turned to study and, at 41 years of age, she was finally able to fully retire from sport and became a certified Master Results Coach, a Trainer and Practitioner of Neuro-Linguistic Programming and Certified Hypnotist.

Annette now serves as an International Trainer for Christopher Howard Training Inc, and creates her own coaching and teaching projects with her businesses, Annetteffect and Success beyond Sport. She specializes in improving athletes' mindsets, and in helping teams, businesses and individuals achieve better results in their career, health and relationships.

Annette uses the same tools she shares with clients to transform her own life. With a career that takes her travelling internationally several times a year, she also created an amazing romantic relationship and a home base in Maui, Hawaii. During 2007 and 2008 Annette hit several travel destinations from her wish list - Hawaii, Macchu Piccu, a safari in South Africa, and Cambodia, all the while mingling with other highly successful entrepreneurs and millionaires. Her life today is a testament to the power of self development, a far cry from the unhappy days in her past.

• •

Annette is available for individual and group coaching, speaking engagements, as well as workshops on the Success beyond Sport program. If you need a dynamic speaker for your next event, go to **www.annetteffect.com** to enquire about booking Annette. Audiences love her compelling story and practical tools for self improvement.

You can find further support for your success in the Locker Room at **www.successbeyondsport.com** – an online community created to provide a supportive environment for athletes.

Sign up for the free newsletter and find out about upcoming events.

• • BIO • •

- Master Results Coach & NLP Practitioner
- NLP Trainer
- Master Hypnosis
- 2000 Olympian – Beach Volleyball
- B. Physiotherapy
- Attendee and speaker at 2009 IART Conference (Institute fo Athletes in Retirement and Transition)

Volleyball Career (1983-2007)

BEACH VOLLEYBALL

Olympic Games
Sydney 2000   19th

World Tour Highlights

Highest Ranking	8th - 1994
5th Place finishes	Montreal '02; Puerto Rico '95, Korea '96
6th Place finish	Chile '94
7th Place finishes	USA '94, Japan '97, Portugal '98

Asian Championships

Asian Champion	1995
Runner-up Champion	1994
Tour Wins	Thailand '96, Taipei '95, China '95
Runner Up	Philippines '94, '95; Thailand '94; Hong Kong '95

Invitationals

Tahiti Open Champion	2002
Noumea Open 3rd	2006

Australian Tour Highlights

Australian Open	2nd ('94, '00); 3rd ('93, '95, '96)
Tour Wins	Surfers Paradise '94,'00,
	Perth '94, '98,'00;
	Sydney Championships '98
	Australia Cup '92
Best Defender Award	1998, 2001

New Zealand Tour

New Zealand Champion	1996, '97, '99
Runner-up Champion	1998
Auckland Open Champion	2001, '03
Number of Tour Wins	13

Individual Awards

Queensland State Tour '96, '02	Most Valuable Player Award
	Best Defender Award '96
	Best Server '02
Inducted Queensland Beach Volleyball Hall of Fame	2009
Australian Volleyball Federation	Merit Award 2002

INDOOR VOLLEYBALL

State Representation

Queensland – junior level	1983 – 1986
South Australia – senior level	1986 – 1987
West Australia – senior level	1987 – 1993

National Representation

Youth Team (captain)	1988
Senior Team	1989 – 1993
Asian Championships	1989.'91,'93
World Qualifying Championships	1990
Captain	1993
International Club – The Netherlands	
Delta Lloyd/Amstelveen	1990/91

COMMITTEES/BOARDS

Queensland Volleyball Association Board	2002 – 2006
Asian Beach Volleyball Council	2002 – 2005
West Australian Institute of Sport Board	2001
Australian Beach Volleyball Commission	1996 - 1999
Australian Volleyball	
Professionals Association	1992-1998, 2002
Secretary 1997 –98, '02	
West Australian Volleyball	
Association Board	1989

4398777

Made in the USA
Charleston, SC
14 January 2010